Praise for *Value-Driven Business Process Management*

"The book goes well beyond a traditional methods-and-tools perspective to present the most current, broadly informed view of BPM as a management discipline. Drawing from their extensive experience, Franz and Kirchmer outline the path for using BPM to gain immediate value and benefits across the organization while strengthening strategic capabilities for the long term—arming leaders with both the vision and the practical insights to initiate action. Applying the principles in the book to understand your company's processes in a practical and efficient manner—and how the business processes maximize your value chain—is a critical tool for maximizing what a company should be doing and eliminating the non-value-add processes. It also ensures complete integration of effort throughout the company to achieve the business objectives."

    —**PAUL O'FLAHERTY,** *Finance Director, Eskom*

"Franz and Kirchmer go directly to the heart of the role of BPM in business by focusing on value as the driver, management discipline as the requirement, and translating strategy into execution as the measure of success. Value-Driven BPM is a long journey but the framework provided by these authors sets a map for the first hundred steps along the way."

    —**RICHARD MALTSBARGER,** *SVP of Strategy & BPM, Lowe's Companies, Inc.*

"If your CEO has delivered a set of strategic imperatives, you are ready for Value Driven BPM. This book provides the vision of how to win in the integrated global economy by building a core BPM discipline in your company to simplify the delivery of business strategy. This is your roadmap to business governance of your processes to align all levels of your workforce and business partners and cost-effective application of IT to deliver solutions required in today's business environment. Value-Driven BPM is the approach to gain full transparency to your operations and will deliver a capability in your organization for agile and efficient business transformation. Transform at the speed of market changes with Value-Driven BPM."

    —**KATHLEEN DONAHUE,** *Senior Director of Business Process Management, Pfizer Inc.*

"Business Process Management has continued to evolve as a tool organizations use to effectively and efficiently meet customer demands. What distinguishes this work is the way Franz and Kirchmer draw on their extensive experience and field research to show how BPM can be even more than a tool—with their guidance you can learn how to make BPM a framework that integrates and aligns your organization's people and processes with its strategy."

    —**NATE BENNETT,** *Ph.D., Wahlen Professor of Management, Georgia Tech*

"Business Process Management (BPM) has to be implemented as a management discipline and linked to the strategic imperatives of an organization in order to achieve the best business impact. Franz and Kirchmer show how this can be achieved. They present very practicable approaches which are also from an academic point of view well thought through. I recommend the book to top executives, BPM practitioners as well as the academic world."

> —**PROFESSOR DR. DRS. H.C. AUGUST-WILHELM SCHEER,** *BPM Thought Leader and Entrepreneur*

"Value-Driven Business Process Management can become the new paradigm that takes BPM to the next level. The authors provide a compelling argument for the benefits and innovation of a value-driven approach. Based on their comprehensive experiences and related research, they share countless examples and guidelines that will inspire BPM professionals around the globe and across all industries."

> —**PROFESSOR MICHAEL ROSEMANN,** *Head of School, Information Systems School, Science and Engineering Faculty, Queensland University of Technology*

"*Value-Driven Business Process Management* is a game-changing book. Similar to how General Systems Theory improves understanding of the complex nature of organizations, Franz and Kirchmer have shown how a value-based organizing framework for BPM enables practitioners and scholars to significantly improve how modern organizations can effectively link thinking, planning, strategy and execution."

> —**LARRY M. STARR,** *PhD, Executive Director and Academic Chair, Organizational Dynamics Graduate Studies, University of Pennsylvania*

"Franz and Kirchmer provide a strong foundation for readers in every phase of their BPM life cycle."

> —**ALAN TREFLER,** *Founder and CEO, Pegasystems Inc.*

"Value-driven BPM, as defined by Franz and Kirchmer, is an insightful way to use the available methods and tools to get real business impact through process management. It is a fresh approach to quickly move from strategy into execution."

> —**DR. WOLFRAM JOST,** *CTO, Software AG*

VALUE-DRIVEN
BUSINESS PROCESS MANAGEMENT

The Value-Switch
for Lasting
Competitive Advantage

Peter Franz
Mathias Kirchmer

New York Chicago San Francisco Lisbon London Madrid Mexico City
Milan New Delhi San Juan Seoul Singapore Sydney Toronto

1 2 3 4 5 6 7 8 9 0   LPI/LPI   1 9 8 7 6 5 4 3

ISBN   978-0-07-182592-4
MHID   0-07-182592-4

McGraw-Hill Education books are available at special quantity discounts to use as premiums and sales promotions or for use in corporate training programs. To contact a representative, please visit the Contact Us pages at www.mhprofessional.com.

To Monica and Judy, with thanks for your patience and support

Contents

Preface

The journey to mastery of any complex and subtle practice is somewhat of a mystery. Whether it is an investor seeking to "buy low and sell high" or a musician looking to bring a piece of music to life, there is a level of compliance with the instructions, and then a level of virtuosity may follow. Millions are following the path, but only a handful will emerge to become the Warren Buffett or Miles Davis of their generation. How did the masters get there? Most of the time, they can't tell you. Read your Graham and Dodd. Practice.

So it is in business as well. In our profession as management consultants, we have spent our careers in pursuit of a deeper understanding of how to systematically improve management practices. Our version of "buy low, sell high" is called *value-driven business process management (BPM)*. The companies that we've guided in adopting this approach are putting process at the heart of business problem solving and competitiveness, using it to realize immediate benefits while establishing a path for stronger and more strategic capabilities in the long term. For instance, a major oil and gas company used value-driven BPM to deliver the benefits of postmerger integration faster than anticipated while enhancing core safety and compliance—an application of the tenets discussed in this book that was not only worth tens of millions to the company but also continues to reduce the risk of plant closures in the future. In another instance, a high-tech company used value-driven BPM to define the focused investments required to increase its production capacity by a factor of 10. The company achieved this expanded capacity at a reduced cost and over a shorter period of time than anticipated, while establishing the skills to continuously improve its process management far into the future.

We have contributed to the development of value-driven BPM across more than two decades, working in various ways to systematize a process-focused approach to management. This book is the result of our journey. In the following pages, we have endeavored to tell the story of what value-driven BPM is, how it works, and how your organization can adopt it as a management discipline to achieve enduring differentiation and superior performance. If you are a business leader who is looking to allow and encourage every single person in the company to express his or her virtuosity in a way that is aligned with strategy, this book is for you—indeed, we hope it will be of great value to BPM practitioners and academics alike. Our goal is to share the knowledge we have gained so that a wider audience can benefit.

We have tried to take much of the mystery out of the journey to high performance and to show how to organize a business so that the execution of processes at all levels reflects the strategic intent of senior management. There are many important contributors to high performance: a deep understanding of capital and how it is deployed; a dynamic ability to adapt the physical operations of the organization; innovation in products to meet changing customer requirements; and many more. Process is then the channel for ensuring that your people and technology can quickly adapt to execute the new paradigm with excellence and, thus, realize the value. We are confident that by understanding the current context and capabilities of BPM and applying the approach outlined in this book—learning to manage your company using what we call the Process of Process Management—you will greatly accelerate progress toward executing and improving your strategy.

One question usually crops up right away in our engagements: "How is value-driven BPM different from plain old BPM, which I've been hearing about for years and on which we have spent a bunch of money?" Value is the answer. Value is the true north that is always present in our approach and that ensures you do not get lost in the technological or methodological weeds. By always keeping value in mind, the tools and methods you have already invested in may be used to support strategy, rather than become an end unto themselves. The companies we have worked with have found that they are transformed from being stuck to being free. While it's ideal to have a CEO like Jack Welch to drive continuous improvement initiatives like Lean Six Sigma, such involvement is rare and much-needed. Value-driven BPM gets the job done at a strategic level, creating the broad context and focus that enable you to get the needed buy-in that a continuous-improvement program alone typically cannot obtain.

The term "value switch" in the subtitle of this book has three essential meanings:

- It means switching your view to an updated appreciation of BPM and its ability to drive value. We have not invented a new form of business process management—instead, we reveal how you can move past the legacy view to the most current, powerful, output-driven view.
- "Making the value switch" means switching your whole organization to an emerging management discipline that is proving to be enormously successful. We share the stories of our work with leading companies that have reshaped their approach by applying the ideas and frameworks presented here.
- And finally, applying value-driven BPM is like "throwing the value switch"—and—as one of the executives interviewed in our research phrased it—"turning the light switch on" across the company. That's because this approach to BPM delivers the benefit of heightened transparency, providing greater visibility into the health of and relationship between key processes. This transparency, in turn, can help you to select appropriate process improvement approaches and point them at the right processes. Heightened transparency is also the key to improving your company's ability to respond successfully to changes and challenges—for example, by knowing which processes produce which costs; by knowing how to decrease costs and quickly implement changes that can have a bottom-line impact; or knowing how best to respond to new trends.

We tell the story of value-driven BPM in three parts.

Part I (Chapters 1–5) focuses on the top-down view. We explain how value-driven BPM can help you increase transparency, evaluate process maturity, identify threats to execution of strategy, set priorities, and then increase process effectiveness and efficiency in a sustainable manner. We wrote Part I specifically for the C-suite executive who wants the full context and the overarching insight to direct change: from the context and details about launching the management discipline of value-driven BPM into action to synchronizing value-driven BPM with existing BPM efforts.

Part II (Chapters 6–8) contains the bottom-up view. Each of the chapters addresses a specific challenge that will need to be faced when value-driven BPM is adopted, such as technology, organizational structure, and change management. Part II will be helpful to those practitioners who are implementing changes, as well as C-level executives responsible for this effort.

Part III (Chapters 9–10) examines value-driven BPM in practice through in-depth case studies and looks at the implications and the future of value-driven BPM. How will value-driven BPM change the C-suite, the world of technology, the way that management is practiced?

We would like to thank the many clients who have both benefited from and added to our body of knowledge as this book took shape, as well as the colleagues who have walked this path with us and provided inspiration along the way. The powerful combination of deep execution excellence, process automation, and the BPM discipline, delivered in an integrated way—focused on value—has shaped much of our thinking.

We would also like to thank Karl-Heinz Floether and Mark Foster for their visionary support for the direction we have taken, as well as the Operations Consulting leadership at Accenture—Mark Pearson, Mark George, and Greg Cudahy—for their review of the manuscript and invaluable contribution.

Our journey to value-driven BPM is ongoing. As we explain in the pages to follow, this management discipline will continue to increase in importance, and we are likely to add to this current body of knowledge through updated editions in the future. We hope you will keep pace with us on this rewarding journey.

Peter Franz, London
Dr. Mathias Kirchmer, Philadelphia
March 1, 2012

VALUE-DRIVEN
BUSINESS PROCESS MANAGEMENT

PART I

Strategy and Planning for Value-Driven BPM

CHAPTER 1

Value-Driven BPM: Why You Need It Now

During our more than four decades of combined experience advising business leaders in the area of business process management, we have had the privilege of meeting with executive teams at companies all over the world. While there are vast differences between industries and countries, we find commonality in the struggle to address a variety of vexing questions. Around the globe, CEOs and senior management teams are asking themselves:

- How can we better align execution with strategy?
- How can we focus our management efforts on the most important problems?
- How can we increase transparency in the most important areas of our business?
- How can we improve our agility in adapting to new market conditions?
- When is incremental improvement enough? When do we need fundamental business transformation?

We have found that, by applying the management discipline we have developed—which we call value-driven BPM—the companies we work with have been able to make immediate and lasting improvements. This approach continuously translates strategy into execution via an organization's processes, delivering sustainable value.

Value-driven business process management (BPM) is the management discipline that uses process as the critical link to translate business *strategy* into *execution*. It sets the right focus for initiatives based on the strategic imperatives of an organization and converts business processes into real *assets* that provide competitive advantage. Value-driven BPM makes business processes more *adaptable*, enabling more agility in adjusting strategy in response to the dynamic business environment.

Gradually, the frustration that companies have experienced in the past falls away, replaced by excitement about the increased ability to master complexity.

In this book we cover value-driven BPM from top to bottom, with the goal of helping you improve your organization's game using the power of process. In this first chapter, we set the context for a more advanced way of applying BPM. We discuss:

- The forces that have converged to drive a need for a new approach to BPM; and
- The decades of evolution that have made this new management discipline possible.

The following chapter completes the contextual picture with a discussion of:

- The positive impact value-driven BPM can have on your company; and
- How you can start your journey toward value-driven BPM.

If you look at how BPM is employed today, efforts range from implementing process automation systems to plugging in modeling tools and populating a repository, to performing enterprise application integration or applying principles of enterprise architecture. The most common problem is that BPM, until now, has consisted of bits and pieces. Effectively, value-driven BPM superimposes a framework on top of all the bits and pieces, organizing them into a cohesive whole.

The benefits of applying value-driven BPM have been researched in a study conducted collaboratively between Accenture, the

Queensland University of Technology in Brisbane (Australia), and the University of Pennsylvania in Philadelphia (USA). As revealed in the initial report from this joint research,[1] discussed in greater detail in Chapter 2, the first benefit of value-driven BPM is a broad increase in transparency. In other words, it disperses the fog of business so that real problems emerge and can be scrutinized.

The next major benefit of value-driven BPM is the ability to reduce the trade-offs inherent in business. Rather than sacrifice quality for efficiency (or vice versa), successful companies find a way to increase quality while increasing efficiency. Similarly, they find ways to be more agile while maintaining compliance. They find ways to tightly integrate people along with processes while managing large, distributed partner ecosystems. Value-driven BPM is an approach with tremendous power to reduce trade-offs in ways that are differentiating.

Some other key findings of our research:

* BPM initiatives without firm support from senior executives and a sense of urgency often focus on methodological and technical issues and become activity-based programs. Value-driven BPM moves the conversation to a higher, more strategic level. The approach first focuses on value and outcomes, then provides the linkages between these strategic imperatives and a company's processes.
* BPM initiatives tend to be executed based on a general methodology and are often not tailored to specific values that matter. Value-driven BPM helps identify those values and connect them to supporting processes quickly and accurately.

In his book *Winning*, former CEO of General Electric Jack Welch describes how he chose to adopt the Six Sigma quality improvement methodology.[2] After 14 years as CEO, Welch was famous for his aggressive stance against stifling bureaucracy and inefficiency. Welch chose Six Sigma as a way to continue and accelerate his war to eliminate waste, foster innovation, and create more value.

Today you may find yourself in the same position Welch was in then. You have tried many ways to improve performance. Some have worked, some have failed, but none has been widely applicable and consistently effective. You may lead a complex organization born from organic growth and an amalgam of mergers and acquisitions.

You may have spent significant time and resources developing strategy, only to find it difficult to get the organization to execute that strategy. This frustration is evident at both a macro and micro level, in large companies and small, all around the globe.

If Welch were a CEO today—if he had spent 14 years making his organization better, but still wanted to increase performance—we believe that the comprehensive approach to value-driven BPM outlined in this book would be the right management discipline to achieve those goals and move to a higher level. Value-driven BPM is valid whether you are starting the journey or are at a more advanced stage.

THE PERFECT STORM: FORCES THAT DEMAND A NEW APPROACH

A "perfect storm" of forces is driving executives to undertake the same search for a new way forward. Business conditions are increasingly complex and risk-prone, demanding more sophisticated forms of optimization. The pace of change has accelerated to the extent that stable equilibrium is an anachronism. Constant change is the new normal. Technology offers choice that has expanded by orders of magnitude. Keeping track of this continuously evolving portfolio of technology capabilities while meeting changing business needs is a fundamental requirement for CIOs. After two decades of research and practice, BPM methods and technology are now ripe to be orchestrated to support a new management discipline that meets these challenges.

When competing in world-class sailing, the seasoned sailor would see more turbulent weather as an opportunity to excel—thus, our use of the contradictory phrase "the perfect storm." In business, too, it is those who can weather turbulent change who will rise to create sustainable advantage.

Business Forecast: Accelerating Change, Increased Risk, Greater Complexity

The first force demanding a new management discipline is the roiling seas of the modern business world. At Accenture we are constantly surveying the landscape for forces that are going to have a long-term impact on strategy. As we do so, we are often asked, "When will things get back to 'normal'?" If "normal" means "the way things were before the last big economic downturn," the answer is, "never." The latest Accenture analysis has identified seven distinct forces that promise to keep life interesting for executives throughout the next decade:

- Population growth
- Changes in technology
- Challenges in energy markets
- Environmental concerns
- Health and terrorism risks
- Uncertain financial markets
- Globalization

The Impact of Rapid Change

Rapid change increases the need for value-driven BPM.[3]

The latest trends in *population growth* indicate that the current global population of 7 billion will rise to 9.3 billion by 2050.[4] One implication is the emergence of a large middle class in Asia, which will represent a huge consumer market. In addition, people above the age of 60 will comprise more than 20 percent of the population.[5] Most of this population growth will occur in cities, which will have to grow to absorb the impact. All three of these population trends will have a dramatic effect on many markets.

Changes in *technology* will accelerate. Right now more than 4 billion people have mobile phones,[6] a number that will increase, especially in emerging markets. Mobile payment services will also grow dramatically, changing how consumers spend money. Chips will continue to gain power, allowing real-time processing of information from sensors and smart buildings. Immense growth is expected in health-care technology as well.

The challenge in *energy markets* is finding a sustainable way to support economic growth. Renewable sources of energy will be in great demand, and technologies like the smart grid will be used to make energy delivery more efficient and responsive to changes in the costs of production.

Environmental concerns will focus on achieving sustainable growth without damaging the ecosystem. Restrictions on carbon will have to be managed, and food and water will become scarcer, more carefully managed resources.

Health and terrorism risks will likely feature prominently in the next decade. Epidemics like the SARS outbreak will recur, terrorism will continue to disrupt society, and other unforeseen risks are also likely.

> The turmoil in the *financial markets* in which credit dried up in a flash could easily be repeated. The reform of financial markets will continue as states, businesses, and civil society learn to work together in a networked world. The effect of this evolution on business will be tremendous.
>
> The interconnectedness brought about by *globalization* has resulted in a world far more synchronized than at any time in history. While this enables greater efficiency, it also means that disruptions from protectionism and natural disasters are more widely felt.

As the pace of change accelerates, these trends suggest that the future will present CEOs and managers with an optimization challenge of unprecedented complexity. Previous management paradigms will be put to the test, and many will not pass. In our opinion, successful approaches to managing a more complex world will require a dramatic extension of transparency and a process-centric management discipline of the sort value-driven BPM provides.

Diversified, Distributed, Consumable Technology

The second force driving companies to seek a new management discipline is the way that the technology landscape is changing to make technology simpler but the task of aligning it with business more complex. Cloud computing, software as a service, and the explosion of specialized devices have afforded businesses greater technological capabilities and more flexibility than ever before. It has become easier for business users to craft technology solutions with limited participation from IT. In addition, the cost of computing power continues to drop while performance skyrockets.

Businesses can buy technology in smaller chunks that are simpler to operate. The days of the massive integrated single-application suite are giving way to a collection of smaller, simpler applications that can be extended through offerings purchased in an app store or sourced over the Internet. Google Apps, Box.net, and Salesforce .com are just a few companies that use this approach to create an ecosystem to promote innovation around their applications. Even large system vendors such as SAP and Oracle are providing access to their applications in smaller, bite-size components that are more easily configurable. The cloud is further changing the sourcing of various layers of IT, from underlying infrastructure through entire processes.

Value-driven BPM provides a filter. The relevance of an individual technology can be determined by asking, "Which technology do we need to improve specific processes?" The clarity provided by such an analysis helps answer difficult questions, such as

* Which assets should be outsourced? Which should be run internally?
* Which should be retired?
* Most important, which are creating the most value?

IT will increasingly use a process framework as the way to organize the application landscape. It has no other choice that will work. We hear evidence of the demand for a rational process framework all the time. One CIO in the financial services industry recently commented, "My application portfolio is getting so diverse, it's almost impossible to keep track of." Value-driven BPM can also organize analysis of business issues and help you understand how they can be resolved using new technologies.

The challenge for your business is assembling all of the diverse, distributed, and easy-to-consume technology into a coherent form tailored to meet your needs. Companies with clarity in their process landscapes can evaluate the role of current and new technology with precision. A process-centric approach provides an organizing framework that speeds decision making.

BPM Comes of Age

The third force enabling the emergence of a new management discipline is the evolution of BPM capabilities. After two decades of research and practice, BPM tools, standards, best practices, and reference models have gone through battle testing. The result is a large collection of technology that includes business process management systems (BPMS), process modeling and repository tools, and a wide collection of industry reference models. These tools, along with targeted process improvement methods, such as Six Sigma, Lean, and Total Quality Management, have gone through cycles of evolution, as companies and practitioners learned how to make them work effectively.

These tools all represent pieces of the puzzle of a comprehensive, process-centric management discipline. Value-driven BPM brings all of this learning together into a systematic form that helps meet the challenges facing modern management teams. The rest of this chapter and Chapter 2 explain exactly how.

THE MANAGEMENT DISCIPLINE OF VALUE-DRIVEN BPM

When we first sit down with an executive team to discuss the challenges facing a business and how value-driven BPM might help, we often hear statements like these:

- "Why do we need BPM? We have more important things to deal with."
- "BPM is too expensive; we can't afford it."
- "We have ERP. That's our BPM."
- "We already have BPM. I signed off on software last year."
- "We've been doing Six Sigma. Isn't that BPM?"
- "We have a BPM team to look after process. Why do you want management involved?"

Our first task in most conversations is drawing a sharp distinction between what an organization has come to think of as BPM and the practical management discipline of value-driven BPM. It turns out that the legacy of BPM as it has been practiced for more than 20 years is sometimes a liability when explaining value-driven BPM to companies for the first time. Many may not even recognize the problems in the statements above.

To clearly understand how value-driven BPM differs from other process-focused approaches such as Lean Manufacturing, Total Quality Management, Business Process Reengineering, and Six Sigma (a topic we cover in more detail in Chapter 5), we will build our definition from the bottom up. Each of these process improvement methods in its basic form offers a way of thinking and an implied scope. Lean Manufacturing, for example, was first applied in an industrial context and then applied in service-oriented companies. Value streams are identified, work processes are standardized, and waste is squeezed out of a system through a series of incremental steps. Six Sigma focuses on finding sources of variability in processes and systematically eliminating them. Business Process Reengineering focuses on detailed reviews of problems in "as-is" processes to define improved "to-be" states for those processes. Techniques such as *Kaizen* are effective at engaging a large number of people in process improvement. There are numerous examples of projects using these techniques delivering significant value when executed in the right context. The common denominator in all these projects is the end-to-end focus on value and the parallel emphasis on process execution excellence while creating the ongoing process management discipline. Value-driven BPM has emerged as the discipline to have a more structured approach to focusing on value, driving execution excellence, and sustaining this achievement over time.

Various kinds of technology were developed to support BPM: Process modeling environments and repositories allowed organizations to describe their business from top to bottom. Process reference models were created to capture standard industry practices. Business process management systems allowed software to be constructed using process descriptions as a foundation. Business activity monitoring systems allowed detailed monitoring of end-to-end processes. Much attention has been paid to the graphical representation of processes. Process modeling was used to design integration between applications or to configure applications themselves. The latest development is the field of social BPM, in which social media techniques are applied to process management.

Great strides were made in both process improvement methods and technology, but one problem consistently arose. Often, process improvement methods made business processes more efficient without sufficient connection to the company's core value-creating mission. BPM technology would be used to create ornate models, only to find that the models were rarely referenced.

BPM as it has been practiced up to now has fallen short of its potential. A powerful set of tools has been developed for focusing on processes. But for BPM to be a management discipline, it needs to focus on affecting business outcomes and on how the business creates value. Value-driven BPM adds the missing pieces that transform BPM into a management discipline that is taking its rightful place alongside Finance, Accounting, HR, and other mature management practices.

Focused on Business Outcomes

One of the key differences between BPM as it has been practiced and value-driven BPM concerns the ambition of the approach. BPM, in its many forms, is mostly defined as a way to improve a process. BPM has little to say about how to select the process to improve, or about how to connect processes to strategy. These issues are discussed in most descriptions of BPM, but the methods themselves do not really address them.

> Some of the most effective questions we ask BPM leaders in an organization are, "What value do you deliver?" and "How do you justify your existence to a CEO?" The range of responses is quite diverse. Sometimes we are told, "I look after the process models," but it's unclear why the process models need attention in the first place.

Value-driven BPM adds the missing elements needed to achieve the level of a management discipline as shown in Figure 1-1. It systematically transfers business processes into process assets that provide competitive advantage to an organization. A management discipline has the business as its primary focus. The strategy, the technology, and the people are all kept in mind as you apply value-driven BPM. All of the methods and tools of traditional BPM are included in the life cycle of value-driven BPM, but they are orchestrated more effectively.

Executives sometimes find it odd that we spend the first part of our initial meeting with them talking about the business strategy, the market environment, and the enduring challenges they face, instead of speaking about processes. Often, they ask, "When are we going to discuss processes and BPM?" Our answer is always the same: "After we have a better understanding of your business and the challenges it faces—and by the way, we are already talking about BPM."

Definition of a Management Discipline

In Gartner's IT Glossary, BPM is defined as "a management discipline that treats business processes as assets that directly improve enterprise performance by driving operational excellence and business agility."[7]

Gartner's definition is on target, but it leaves one term insufficiently clarified: management discipline.

A management discipline is a set of practices for managing risks and ensuring success with respect to a key function that is crucial to a company's success. A management discipline focuses on the big picture and the details, providing a point of view about how a specific area of a company should work. In the end, a management discipline ensures that a particular function contributes the maximum amount to the rest of the business in a way that continuously improves.

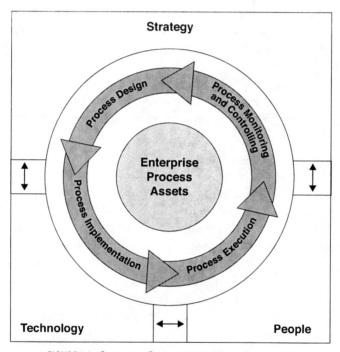

FIGURE 1-1. Organizing Framework for Value-Driven BPM

(After Mathias Kirchmer, High-Performance Through Process Excellence, 2nd ed., Berlin: Springer-Verlag, 2011)

Applies to Every Part of the Organization

A true management discipline is characterized not only by a focus on business outcomes but also by its universal applicability. We find that this concept is one of the most challenging to get across, but it is the key to understanding the difference between BPM and value-driven BPM.

In most businesses, certain functions are used by every part of the business. Human Resources, for example, has a process for hiring and terminating employees, for providing benefits, for resolving disputes, and for handling any other events that occur in the course of employment. The finance department provides a set of budgeting and accounting practices, a process for making a capital allocation request, and mechanisms to spend and collect money.

One of the central insights of value-driven BPM is that every part of the company needs a Process of Process Management, which we describe in great detail in Chapter 3. The Process of Process Management is the way that value-driven BPM comes to life in every part of an organization. It is a reference model for putting value-driven BPM to work, by defining governance, management, and operational processes.

Value-Driven BPM and the Process of Process Management

This book uses two terms to speak about the same body of knowledge. When we use the term *value-driven BPM*, we are talking about the entire body of knowledge, not only of what the authors have added but also of the practices and technology that have been developed under the general umbrella of BPM for the past 20 years.

When we use the term *Process of Process Management*, we are talking about how this body of knowledge is organized into processes for putting value-driven BPM to work in a company. The Process of Process Management, like value-driven BPM, includes all of the practices and technology of BPM but also adds new processes for BPM operations that are used to coordinate the use of BPM at a company. In other words, value-driven BPM is the name for the black box. The Process of Process Management is the name for the workings inside of the black box.

The term *BPM* refers to all the developments that have led to the creation of value-driven BPM and the Process of Process Management. BPM is included in and encompassed by value-driven BPM and the Process of Process Management.

For example, in the HR department, the tools of value-driven BPM, which include all the tools and practices of traditional BPM, can be used to define the processes and capture the definitions in process repositories. The captured processes can then be compared to reference models, instrumented with metrics, and analyzed using process improvement methods. Value-driven BPM also employs qualitative analysis to determine the maturity of the processes and their relation to value creation in a business. This qualitative analysis can be used to determine which processes should be given priority for improvement. Chapter 4 goes into great detail about how to evaluate processes and create a roadmap.

We find that the legacy of BPM gets in the way of understanding this point. The Process of Process Management is not a way to run one project in isolation. It is a way to provide governance, monitoring, evaluation, and improvement for all processes in the company that need attention. Just as every department works with HR, every department should also work with a department that is in charge of how processes are run. It doesn't matter if a Center of Excellence is created as a resource or a Chief Process Officer is put in charge (a scenario we will discuss in more detail in Chapter 10), everyone in the business should be able to use the Process of Process Management to improve his or her performance using central experts as a resource for guidance and governance.

Constructed for Lasting Impact

It is vital to remember that adopting value-driven BPM is more than just putting in place tools, techniques, and content, which are typically starting points. Value-driven BPM is also about much more than putting a repository in place. It's about adopting a new way of thinking, making people explicitly responsible for process, and making sure that the assets you use are linked to the activities people actually perform. This new way of thinking is what we call a *process-centric culture*. It's not just a functional library that runs in the background. It is the heartbeat of the organization.

In a process-centric culture, there is a shared awareness about how process organizes the way work gets done, analyzes the work, and helps organizations react to problems. When people in a process-centric culture talk about what they do, they don't just focus on their own tasks. They also talk about the impact the tasks will have on other people involved in the process. They pay attention to detail in their own area with a new understanding about how their mistakes might impact other people. They think in a more customer-oriented way, because they understand clearly how processes result in an overall outcome of value for customers. They also know which processes must be adhered to strictly, because regulatory compliance is an issue, and which processes are more roughly defined and allow more of a degree of freedom to be creative and agile.

One of the most important differences between value-driven BPM and the way BPM has been practiced up until now are practices that focus on institutionalizing behavior and making a lasting impact. The first measure to ensure a lasting impact, and to create a process-centric culture, is to create a Center of Excellence (CoE) as the owner of the Process of Process Management, devoted to promoting its effective use throughout the company. Just as the HR department helps the rest of your company manage personnel and related issues, a CoE will help the rest of your company run the Process of Process Management to deal with all aspects of process management. Adoption of value-driven BPM is never something that happens overnight. The method itself is designed to be gradual. In each step forward, value-driven BPM seeks to improve both the operational processes in a company and the maturity of the Process of Process Management. When a project achieves both goals at once, we call it a triangulation, a concept explored in Chapter 4.

The Constituent Parts of Value-Driven BPM

Establishing ownership of the Process of Process Management in a Center of Excellence is only one step toward ensuring lasting change. For value-driven BPM or any other practice to be embedded in an enduring way, other aspects of your company need to change to support the practice and to make it a permanent part of the way your company works. We have applied the concept of a "capability blueprint," developed by Accenture to create the BPM capability blueprint shown in Figure 1-2. It depicts all of the components that need to be addressed when value-driven BPM is adopted.

The top of the diagram shows organizational components:

- *Organization*: Includes the BPM Center of Excellence and other organizational units dedicated to value-driven BPM. Modes of existence include centralized, decentralized, and hybrid.
- *Competencies or offerings:* The services that the value-driven BPM organization delivers to the rest of the company, such as management of a process repository or assistance in running process improvement projects.

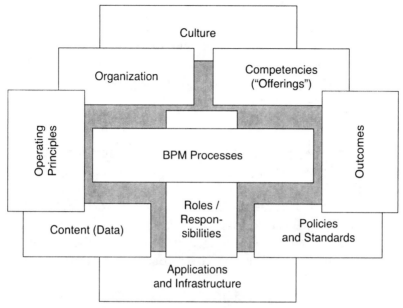

FIGURE 1-2. The BPM Capability Blueprint

(From Mathias Kirchmer, "The Process of Process Management," Accenture BPM Publication, 2011)

- *Culture:* A process-centric management mind-set, focused on end-to-end process thinking.

At the center of the diagram are

- *Roles and responsibilities:* All of the roles necessary to carry out the Process of Process Management.
- *The Process of Process Management:* The set of processes for implementing value-driven BPM, based on all of the other components. It brings all the other components together and aligns them to create business value.

The bottom of the diagram consists of core infrastructure components that should be adapted as value-driven BPM is adopted:

- *Content or data:* Information required by value-driven BPM, for example: process models, value frameworks, and IT frameworks.

- *Applications and infrastructure:* For example, process repository tools or process execution engines.
- *Policies and standards:* Guidelines for operations, methods and tools, delivery, transformation, support, modeling, automation standards, business architecture standards, and so on.

On the sides of the diagram are

- *Operating principles:* The values of the organization that are closely connected to value-driven BPM. These are typically drivers to initiate value-driven BPM in an organization.
- *Outcomes:* The desired business results of processes and improvements made to processes. These are synonymous with the value pairs described in Chapter 2, in the section "Reducing or Resolving Classical Business Conflicts."

Without eventually aligning all of these components to support value-driven BPM, there is a high risk of failure. The alignment happens over time as the implementation of a process-centric culture becomes more complete with every step forward.

As your organization gradually adopts value-driven BPM, you will be simultaneously improving processes and engendering a process-centric culture suffused with pervasive and lasting adoption. *Pervasive adoption* means that hiring processes, organizational structures, training, policies, job roles, culture, supporting technologies and applications, and other standard ways of doing business may need to be changed to be aligned with value-driven BPM. *Lasting adoption* means putting in place a new cultural way of thinking, understanding the organizational implications, making sure everyone understands roles and responsibilities, making it clear what the outcomes are going to be, and establishing how everything is going to operate. Of course, your company also needs to put in place the underlying infrastructure—the content, the data, the tools, the applications, the policy standards, and so on. To achieve enduring success with your organization's Process of Process Management, or any other capability, a leadership team should address all of these concerns. If BPM does not become a way of life, it may not have a lasting impact.

Most of the failed BPM programs we have encountered were done in isolation. For example, repositories were built but never used.

Many of the components in the BPM Capability Blueprint essentially ignored the BPM efforts.

The distinction between BPM as it has been traditionally promoted and value-driven BPM should now be clear. Because it is a management discipline, adopting value-driven BPM means that gradually a process-focused way of thinking permeates the entire organization. Everyone both uses and supports the Process of Process Management in a way that is promoted and governed by the central BPM organization. In Chapter 2, we look at the powerful impact value-driven BPM can have on an organization.

Notes

1. Peter Franz, Mathias Kirchmer, and Michael Rosemann, "Value-Driven Business Process Management: Which Values Matter for BPM," Accenture and Queensland University of Technology, 2011.

2. Jack Welch and Suzy Welch, *Winning* (New York: Harper Collins, 2005).

3. Accenture analysis.

4. United Nations Population Database, 2010.

5. Ibid.

6. United Nations International Telecommunications Union (ITU), 2009.

7. "Business Process Management," Gartner IT Glossary, accessed August 7, 2011, http://www.gartner.com/technology/it-glossary/business-process -management.jsp.

CHAPTER 2

The Impact of Value-Driven BPM

The real test of any management discipline is not how it works in theory, but how it works in practice to address the challenging situations business leaders face. While the impact of value-driven BPM is comprehensive and far-reaching, we can illustrate its potential by looking at three specific ways this new management discipline creates value. In this chapter, we'll examine how value-driven BPM can (1) serve as an organizing principle; (2) help align strategy and execution; and (3) create transparency, which in turn helps to reduce the trade-offs that organizations are typically forced to make.

VALUE AS AN ORGANIZING PRINCIPLE

The secret sauce of value-driven BPM is its focus on value as an organizing principle. The importance of focusing on value cannot be overemphasized. Without it, BPM or any methodology or management practice quickly gets off track as the excitement of embarking on a program of change or using an exciting new method crowds out the focus on business results.

Here's how a focus on value works in practice: The analysis starts by understanding what a business is trying to accomplish. What is the strategy? How has it been translated into business imperatives? What are the value drivers? The understanding created by answering these questions and capturing the answers in formal ways paves the way for a process assessment.

Value-driven BPM employs qualitative assessments of processes (described in Chapter 4) based on rigorous analysis, supported by surveys of executives and analyzed using quantitative measures. The qualitative approach is taken to assess both the maturity of the processes and any qualitative benefits that may come from improving a process. It is important to recognize that not all benefits can be quantified. When possible, metrics for core processes are compared with those of others in the industry and from other industries as well.

Based on the assessment, processes are then sorted into categories. Some processes are core to creating value in the specific company context while others play a supporting role. If a company's performance in a core process falls below the industry level, that process is a prime candidate for improvement. Such processes represent areas of greatest potential return for improvement programs. Often, the results of a value-driven BPM program are measured solely in terms of key performance indicators (KPIs) that reflect desired business outcomes; process metrics are not the focus.

To put it back into a comparative framework, value takes the place of

- Quality in Total Quality Management
- Reduction of waste (and improvement of speed, for example) in Lean Manufacturing
- Reduction of variability to meet customer requirements in Six Sigma

It's fair to note that there are many examples of successful programs that have used these techniques. They would typically have employed many of the value-driven BPM techniques without recognizing them as such. But at the end of the day, driving business value is the most important outcome you are looking for. Focusing on value makes sense to everyone at every level in a company, most of all to CEOs and those trying to drive strategic change. Focusing on value changes how executives think not only about BPM but about everything they do. Value-driven BPM helps focus scarce management time on the most critical process improvement areas. As a management discipline, value-driven BPM shows the way that everyone in the entire organization can participate in creating value.

ALIGNING STRATEGY AND EXECUTION

The focus on value has a significant impact in making clear connections between strategy and execution. Figure 1-1, in Chapter 1, shows how the life cycle of the Process of Process Management, at the center of the graphic, exists within the context of a company's strategy, its technology, and its people.

In a cyclical process, a program of value-driven BPM leads first to a deep understanding of the strategy of a company, its people, and its technology assets, and then to execution of a process life cycle of design, implementation, execution, monitoring, and optimization, centered around a repository of reusable process descriptions and other assets, which enable efficient and effective management of the life cycle. Execution during operations is carried out so that the connection between each process and the strategy is no longer abstract. The outcomes affected by each process are connected to the business imperatives determined by the strategy. The key processes for executing a strategy become clear. Those that matter can get attention, and those that do not can be standardized or outsourced, to be executed at the lowest possible cost. Value-driven BPM transforms strategic intent into people- and IT-based execution.

Because value-driven BPM includes the people and technology aspects of process execution, the process improvement efforts have a lasting effect and become embedded in a company's operations. The Process of Process Management (PoPM) becomes the step-by-step process through which the business is better understood and the most important improvement efforts are identified and executed first, setting the stages for deeper understanding and further progress.

The transparent connection between processes and strategic business imperatives is a huge help during periods of turmoil, when strategy changes. Value-driven BPM helps sort out the complexity of translating strategy to execution in a changing environment. A new strategy means new business imperatives. The processes that help execute those imperatives can quickly become the focus.

The mind-set of value-driven BPM never lets go of value and strategy. The more everyone uses the PoPM, the more deeply strategy and execution are aligned in a business.

CREATING TRANSPARENCY AND REDUCING TRADE-OFFS

Central to the success of value-driven BPM is the power of creating transparency. In the midst of executing strategy, as the puzzle of process, people, and technology is being worked out, companies often face difficult trade-offs:

- How much should be spent optimizing a process?
- How can you become more efficient and cut costs without compromising quality?
- How can you move quickly and adapt to new conditions without breaking compliance regulations?
- How can you create a tightly integrated company but at the same time be open to incorporating partners?

In an effort to understand how value-driven BPM creates value for businesses, we engaged in a research project with the Queensland University of Technology (QUT) in Brisbane, Australia—one of the world's largest academic entities devoted to applied research on BPM—and the Center for Organizational Dynamics at the University of Pennsylvania—a program that provides working professionals with the knowledge, skills, and frameworks to lead organizations and communities in the continuously changing global environment.

Our research examined the way that BPM was applied in a number of industries and the benefits that accrued. The central discovery of the first research report, authored by Accenture and QUT, is the value framework shown in Figure 2-1.

The central and ubiquitous benefit of value-driven BPM is transparency. Only an organization that has a shared understanding of its processes can start reflecting on better ways to design and operate them. By increasing transparency, value-driven BPM in effect makes the trade-offs smaller. The transparency of being able to see the relationships between people, processes, and technology allows for better optimization.[1]

Reducing or Resolving Classical Business Conflicts

Our research identified what might be thought of as the mitigating power of BPM: the power to reduce the trade-offs inherent in business. A well-executed BPM capability offers a surprising advantage by facilitating the simultaneous achievement of seemingly contradictory goals.

Our research identified three sets of such seemingly opposed values, which organizations are typically forced to negotiate:

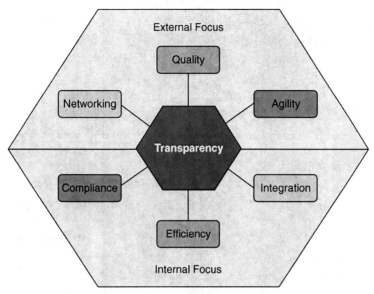

FIGURE 2-1. The Value Framework for Value-Driven BPM

(From Peter Franz, Mathias Kirchmer, and Michael Rosemann, "Value-Driven Business Process Management: Which Values Matter for BPM," Accenture and Queensland University of Technology, 2011)

- *Efficiency/Quality:* A focus on streamlined, highly productive operations *versus* a concentration on customer-focused, quality-driven strategy
- *Compliance/Agility:* The requirement to be highly adaptive and flexible *versus* the increased demand to ensure that operations are conducted predictably and in compliance with standards and regulations
- *Integration/Networking:* Concentrating on integrating employees in the design of processes *versus* networking with external partners and resources

Notice how one term in each pair has an internal focus and the other has an external focus.

Mitigating the Quality/Efficiency Pair

Through the research of Harvard Business School professor Michael Porter and others, it has become commonly accepted that cost and quality are oppositional strategic alternatives.[2] There have been improvements in this over time, and BPM has the potential to help further optimize both.

If an organization is committed to efficiency, it streamlines its business processes by eliminating redundancies and rework. This value driver is at the core of many BPM initiatives and peaked as a motivator during the global economic crisis. Many organizations support efficiency through process improvement techniques, such as Lean Manufacturing, with its focus on eliminating different types of cost-driving waste.

For instance, a shared service organization in Australia initiated a BPM program with the goal of reducing operational expenses by AUS$40 million over four years. Each process redesign project reports its cost-savings potential. The organization deploys activity-based costing and quantifies each process model in terms of its operational costs, which provides transparency.

Improvements in corporate efficiency are in many cases not visible to external stakeholders until they are passed on as price reductions. BPM projects that seek to do "the same for less" can be regarded as having an internal focus.

An efficiency-focused BPM initiative is characterized by the following:

- Strong monetary focus in the analysis and design of processes
- Comparative ranking of processes based on their business value score (i.e., not necessarily monetary)
- Capture of detailed process performance data (including processing time, resource consumption, and resourcing costs)
- Deployment of activity-based costing
- Identification and modeling of cost/complexity drivers
- Detailed tracking of costs related to the Process of Process Management

QIC, one of the largest institutional investment managers in Australia, sees process improvement as a financial investment opportunity. The company calculates a so-called business value score for a process based on various dimensions of strategic relevance, including the inherent financial opportunity. This is an example of linking processes to outcomes of value.

By contrast, aiming toward quality reflects more of an external focus. "Quality" as a BPM value is defined by consumers, who receive products and services as they are delivered by corporate processes. This definition of quality goes far beyond the narrow (engineering-like) specification of products and services and includes, for example, the time it takes to deliver (time-to-market, time-to-order). Thus, quality is the core value that integrates a customer viewpoint into the analysis and design of business processes. Organizations guided by customer-driven quality as a key value will

- Focus on measuring and controlling process performance issues and their root causes
- Embed quality metrics such as customer satisfaction into their processes
- Use relevant Six Sigma and Total Quality Management techniques
- Develop a profound understanding of the interrelationship between process quality and product/service quality
- Define the line of visibility, or the extent of the process that actually is exposed to the customer
- Involve external stakeholders in the Process of Process Management

Our research shows that the last item in particular—the active engagement of external stakeholders in the modeling, analysis, and improvement of business process—is still in its infancy.

Most processes are still described from the viewpoint of the organization as a provider and do not sufficiently consider how they are perceived and valued by external customers. Organizations that make these seemingly superficial changes in semantics actually are setting the course for mitigating traditionally oppositional values.

Examples of integration of external metrics and stakeholders include the following scenarios:

- A bank changed its view from "executing the mortgage process" to "helping customers through the end-to-end process of buying a house."
- A provider of superannuation services changed its focus from "operating business processes" to "determining which

services it could provide" as part of the retirement process in Australia.

- An insurance company analyzed and redesigned its claims-handling processes because of a drop in customer satisfaction. Among other changes, the new process started with customer events such as accidents rather than the first internal event (for example, receiving a customer call). The company identified customer satisfaction as the single most important quality metric for its new claims-handling process.

Mitigating the Compliance/Agility Pair

Transparency helps shrink the trade-off between compliance and agility because processes can be defined faster—increasing agility—and documented and propagated faster as well—increasing compliance.

For example, a health-care provider must stringently adhere to regulations. The Process of Process Management can help design and monitor processes that ensure compliance. If regulations change, the health-care provider has an accurate and up-to-date view of how compliance is actually accomplished and can quickly assess exactly how processes need to change. The transparency provided by the PoPM becomes the foundation for agility by providing a clear, readily accessible starting point for designing new compliance processes. If a new strategy occurs to the health-care provider, the transparency provided by the PoPM enables the changes needed to execute the strategy in a way that maintains compliance.

The same challenge exists at an investment bank that must decide which processes must be precisely defined and monitored to ensure compliance and which processes can be executed with larger degrees of freedom to allow adaptation to market conditions or cross-selling opportunities.

Mitigating the Integration/Networking Value Pair

Organizations tend to have a focus on either internal or external resources. However, unlike the efficiency value driver, the integration/networking value pair in particular highlights the impact of process design on internal and external resources. This pair targets questions such as "How are the processes seen by employees?" and

"What is the external perception of the environmental impact of our processes?"

Integration captures the implications of current or intended process design on employees. This includes questions such as "Will the process lead to rewarding job descriptions?," "Are employees accepting the new process design?," and "Do the process metrics lead to the desired behavior?"

This view of internal integration is supported by the functionality of advanced process repositories that support navigation through complex process landscapes based on roles so that employees see only the processes they need to see.

For example, in the case of a state government department, a BPM initiative was driven by a desire to shape innovative processes and encourage new college graduates to join the organization. In another example, a shared service provider put its employees first in its BPM initiative. Senior executives wanted to make sure that a simple but sufficient set of process documentation was available to employees to provide guidance for their daily work.

A focus on the integration value requires

- Close involvement of employees in process design to ensure acceptance
- Capturing metrics such as employee satisfaction with business processes
- A well-maintained link between process models, operating procedures, and job descriptions
- A decentralized, bottom-up approach toward process improvement

By comparison, organizations that emphasize networking see processes as assets involving external partners and resources. This includes in particular the recent move toward "green" processes. Carbon footprint assessments within a business process capture this value. Another way to calculate the environmental impact of a business process is via activity-based emission (ABE) control. Similar to activity-based costing, ABE assesses the extent to which processes consume certain resources and related emissions.

For example, a medium-size utility company explored BPM as a way to collect data related to emissions from interorganizational supply chain processes. Based on modeling standards and process analysis methodologies, such as Six Sigma, the company designed relevant extensions that facilitated capturing processes' environmental impact.

BPM methodologies need to be able to measure carbon emissions of resources involved in business processes. Networking also encompasses inclusion of customers, suppliers, and any affiliates of the business in the process design effort. All should be carefully integrated to ensure positive synergy and sustainable partner relationships.

The integration of social networking technologies in BPM is an indication that networking continues to be an important value. Complementing BPM systems with features as they are provided, for example, by solutions such as LinkedIn or Twitter, allows organizations to identify relevant resources outside their own boundaries, as well as conveniently inform external stakeholders about status changes during the execution of business processes.

Networking as a driving value for BPM requires that the organization

- Identify the role of external partners and resources in the context of their business processes
- Complement the traditional focus on time, cost, and quality with environmental impact (where relevant)
- Explore the benefits and opportunities of social technologies to engage external stakeholders and resources

The QUT/Accenture research revealed that value-driven BPM can achieve substantial victories by reducing the impact of all these trade-offs. In other words, value-driven BPM has the power of *"and."* With transparency about how your business works *and* how strategy is linked to execution, it becomes possible to have quality *and* efficiency, compliance *and* agility, integration *and* networking. We refer to the power of *and* as the mitigating power of value-driven BPM.

BEGINNING YOUR JOURNEY TOWARD VALUE-DRIVEN BPM

As we discussed in Chapter 1, Jack Welch adopted Six Sigma as a way to systematically improve performance and attack inefficiencies in all of the businesses under the GE umbrella. In essence he declared to

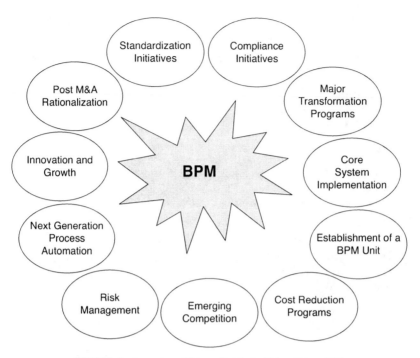

FIGURE 2-2. Examples of Trigger Points for Value-Driven BPM

the company, "Use this method to do your jobs." But in practice, what happened was that Six Sigma was applied on a project-by-project basis while the company grew in its competence to support the method. This is exactly how adoption of value-driven BPM works. Someone declares that it is a promising method and supports its use. Then in each project, not only are operational processes improved using the Process of Process Management but the organizational skill and maturity to execute the PoPM is also improved. (It should be noted that for some organizations a top-down approach is possible, in which a broad organizational capability is developed and then rolled out systematically. Such organizations are the exception in our experience.)

So, if your company is dedicated to value-driven BPM and is taking a gradual approach to implement the PoPM and build an organizational competence, it is wise to be on the lookout for business situations where BPM can provide the most value. We call such projects *trigger points* for the adoption of value-driven BPM. Figure 2-2 shows examples of the most common trigger points we have observed in the field through direct engagement with clients.[3]

This list is not exhaustive but provides a few examples of where value-driven BPM often starts. In Chapter 3, we look at the Process of Process Management in depth and see how any of these triggers may be a starting point on the journey to value-driven BPM for your organization.

Notes

1. Peter Franz, Mathias Kirchmer, and Michael Rosemann, "Value-Driven Business Process Management: Which Values Matter for BPM," Accenture and Queensland University of Technology, 2011.

2. Michael E. Porter, *Competitive Strategy: Techniques for Analyzing Industries and Competitors* (New York: Free Press, 1998).

3. Mathias Kirchmer, "Competitive Advantage in an Era of Change: 11 Typical Business Situations Where Business Process Management Delivers Value," Accenture, 2011.

CHAPTER 3

The Process of Process Management

How do you turn your organization into one that can differentiate on the way it handles and improves processes? In our opinion, based on experience, the best way to do this is to create a process for the way you handle process improvements. We know that the Process of Process Management might sound a bit like the Value of Value or the Business of Business. Bear with us, because the story is far more compelling than you may think. This chapter describes how you can build lasting BPM capabilities that help ensure your work in improving processes is carried forward and can be spread effectively across your organization.

Companies have historically seen BPM as a one-time transformation or improvement project. But the continuous change that typifies today's business environment requires a permanent management discipline that can adjust and improve processes. Value-driven BPM is that discipline, implemented through the Process of Process Management (PoPM). Onetime, project-driven initiatives return temporary results. A built-in discipline for process management builds a sustainable capability for adapting to change and continuously improving or transforming processes at a company.

Your company needs to be able to preserve the gains made when developing new processes and improving existing ones. The competitive value of processes is already well understood, and a myriad of process improvement techniques—Lean, Six Sigma, and Total Quality Management, to name a few—have been used successfully over the years. But, in general, process improvement techniques address only the most tactical layer of the big picture. Importantly, these techniques work from the bottom up and cover only selected aspects of processes—leaving out structural or technology changes, for example. As a consequence, they often don't support larger, structural changes that "bake in" the successes of process improvements. Nevertheless, the appeal of their clean, surgical precision has led to a collective corporate obsession with the "how" of improvement techniques—leaving the "what" and the "why" somewhat in the dust. The big picture is lost, and improvements don't last.

This chapter is organized around our core argument that bringing value to an organization through BPM is a process in itself. The Process of Process Management describes how value-driven BPM is implemented. As such, this process should be defined, implemented, executed, and controlled just like any other business process.

The chapter examines why you need to develop the Process of Process Management to realize the value and benefits of BPM on an ongoing, enterprise-wide basis. We also offer examples of how different companies have successfully approached the development of their own Process of Process Management, illustrating various typical situations and possibilities. We present a reference model to demonstrate all of the moving parts of a Process of Process Management.

Based on this reference model, we give an overview of how and why the various components of the Process of Process Management are critical to generating and sustaining corporate value. The chapter concludes with a discussion of some key factors in making such a Process of Process Management successful.

WHAT IS A PROCESS OF PROCESS MANAGEMENT?

Establishing a Process of Process Management within your organization is the central, most critical aspect of achieving value-driven BPM, as successful businesses are increasingly coming to appreciate. A process approach to BPM leads to the systematic definition and rollout of a BPM capability, and accounts for its own ongoing management, because—like any other process—it needs to be organized and proactively managed.

The Process of Process Management only makes sense if an organization has committed to a process-focused management philosophy. For the PoPM to work, a company will already have come to the conclusion that defining, tracking, and optimizing processes are fundamental to success. Once that mind-set is in place, the question is how to apply it. The PoPM provides tremendous help in

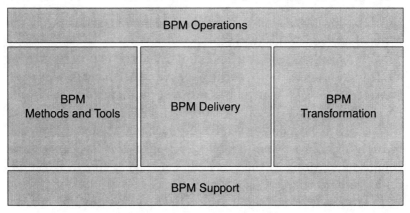

FIGURE 3-1. Accenture Process Reference Model for PoPM (basic version)

answering that question in the context of a specific company's strategy and operations.

So far, so good. Now let's move to a slightly higher level of thinking. The PoPM is a process itself. A process, by definition, delivers a result of value. The value delivered by the PoPM is strategic in that the processes in your company are more transparent, can be optimized in a targeted manner, and are explicitly aligned with strategy. The PoPM can also be applied tactically to help improve all the processes used to run a department or a division. In other words, the PoPM works on two levels: it improves specific operational processes *and* it improves your ability to understand, prioritize, and manage processes.

To guide you in establishing a Process of Process Management, we have developed a reference model that is applicable to any industry or business[1]. It captures all of the basic, BPM-related activities and subprocesses that lead to value for the enterprise. We will discuss the subprocesses in greater detail later in this chapter. First, let's look at the major areas of activity.

As shown in Figure 3-1, the PoPM consists of five major process areas:

- BPM Operations
- BPM Methods and Tools
- BPM Delivery
- BPM Transformation
- BPM Support

The following summary illuminates the breadth and depth of the material covered in this reference model:

BPM operations reflects a high-level management process, akin to strategy management or enterprise performance management. The perspective for BPM operations processes is that of a leader of the entire organization. BPM operations processes are at the heart of what is new about value-driven BPM, which is a systematic approach to business improvement. BPM operations is the "process central command." It provides the overall direction, keeps the focus on priorities, and manages the agents of change.

Below it, the three "service towers" of process capability implement changes through the functional tools and infrastructure. The bottom rung, BPM support, consists of shared services that keep the organization functioning.

BPM methods and tools encompasses much of what has traditionally been thought of as BPM. Methods and tools include repositories, modeling tools, and the application of Six Sigma, Lean, Total Quality Management, and other improvement methods. Notice how this component, whose constituent parts have been very prominent in discussions of BPM in the past, is only one part of value-driven BPM.

BPM delivery includes the rest of what has been known as BPM, that is, the delivery approach for process strategy, analysis, design, implementation, execution, and monitoring. In value-driven BPM, this approach is applied in a much richer context that takes into account strategy as well as operational and PoPM process maturity.

BPM transformation encompasses the cultural, change management, and project management methods that need to be applied to effect lasting change in any organization. BPM community, included in this tower, refers to the community of practice that is created in a Center of Excellence and propagated to the rest of the organization.

BPM support refers to how the rest of the company plays a role in supporting the implementation of the PoPM. Finance, HR, IT, and other areas should participate and adapt to make the PoPM successful.

WHY YOU NEED A PROCESS OF PROCESS MANAGEMENT

How can establishing a Process of Process Management help drive value at an organization? On the surface, it may seem like just another process improvement technique, but as Chapter 1 describes, value-driven BPM is a management discipline, and its success depends on establishing a Process of Process Management. Is there an easier way? Is there another way? In our experience in engagements with hundreds of clients, we haven't yet found another way that is as effective.

As discussed previously, you can think of value-driven BPM like any other management discipline that applies throughout the company, such as human resources (HR). HR thinking and practices pervade every department in the company, because every department has people. Instruments of HR, such as performance evaluations, are based on defined HR processes and then executed for all departments. Similarly, every department has processes. Processes require top-level leadership along with assets that need to be nurtured and developed, just like people (employees) and IT (hardware and software). Value-driven BPM and the PoPM deliver business process management services to the entire organization in the same way HR delivers personnel management services.

Why do you need a Process of Process Management to make value-driven BPM happen?

* To focus management attention on the most critical process areas
* To align process improvement initiatives around strategic priorities
* To be able to react quickly to business change and resulting process requirements
* To decide when to make incremental changes and when to execute larger transformations
* To make process management part of the whole organization
* To add pace and certainty to process improvement initiatives
* To transfer successes from one part of the organization to another
* To define roles and responsibilities and develop the right skills
* To focus the use of BPM methods and tools on value creation
* To ensure lasting solutions to process approaches
* To make BPM successes repeatable
* To sustain BPM efforts
* To communicate clearly what the organization gets from BPM and when it makes sense for employees to request BPM support

A REFERENCE MODEL FOR THE PROCESS OF PROCESS MANAGEMENT

The Accenture Process Reference Model helps companies define, implement, and maintain a Process of Process Management. The basic view of the model was shown in Figure 3-1. Figure 3-2 shows this model with its subprocesses.

This reference model offers a basic, cross-industry description of a general Process of Process Management that you can easily adjust for your specific organization. It captures all the BPM-related activities and subprocesses that, when combined, deliver the defined value. Each subprocess can be thought of as a point of entry into the operating model of value-driven BPM. Remember, no company implements every part of the reference model. The right approach is to find the parts that work to create a PoPM that is effective for the needs of your organization. Also keep in mind that any grand vision of a PoPM is usually implemented gradually by adopting a few practices, making them successful, and then expanding. In other words, don't be daunted by the breadth and depth of the reference model.

Now we turn in more detail to the five major process areas and their subprocesses.

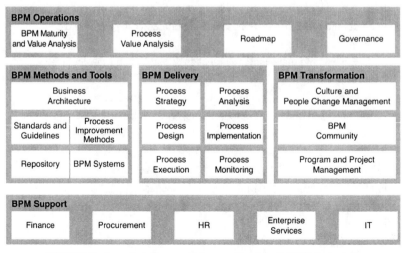

FIGURE 3-2. Accenture Process Reference Model for PoPM (full version)

BPM Operations

BPM operations is the key to getting the right foundation in place to successfully implement value-driven BPM. It is the brain, the cerebral cortex, of value-driven BPM.

In BPM operations, practitioners analyze existing processes, prioritize processes for improvement, create a roadmap for implementing those improvements, and set in place a form of governance for roles, responsibilities, and accountability of personnel who will be responsible for keeping the operational processes and BPM on track—and getting things done. In practice, BPM operations is often the starting point of the BPM journey, and it comprises the initial activities of a BPM Center of Excellence.

Questions BPM operations can answer:

- Which processes currently provide the most value?
- Which processes should we prioritize for improvement?
- What are the high-impact, low-maturity processes?
- Who should be responsible for establishing and maintaining value-driven BPM?
- What are we doing to further develop a lasting BPM capability?
- Which processes should be locally governed, and which should be centrally administered?
- What is the business case for each proposed process improvement?
- Which BPM capabilities do I have in place, and which new ones do I have to build?

BPM operations encompasses four subprocesses that provide the context for an ongoing focus on value-driven BPM: BPM maturity and value analysis, process value analysis, creation of a roadmap, and governance.

BPM Maturity and Value Analysis

BPM maturity and value analysis enables practitioners to understand the strength and maturity of current BPM capabilities—for example, your ability to analyze, design, and measure processes, to define key performance indicators, to establish process owners, and the like.

Questions BPM maturity and value analysis can answer:

• Which capabilities do we need to add to meet our goals?
• Where are the biggest gaps in our BPM capability?
• How do we progress in building our BPM capability?

To perform this analysis, practitioners conduct a maturity analysis based on the BPM Capability Blueprint described in Chapter 1 (see Figure 1-2). You can assess your current BPM capabilities—how mature they are and where to improve them—or build additional capabilities to meet your goals.

Additionally, there are several capability assessment models on the market, including those from the Object Management Group (OMG), industry analysts, and academic institutions, such as the Queensland University of Technology in Brisbane, Australia. Accenture has consolidated several models, added its own experiences, and structured its reference model based on the BPM Capability Blueprint.

Having defined your BPM capability, you now need to be clear on the outcomes you seek. If you don't do this, you will be lost on where to go next. As one CIO told us, "It's like being all dressed up and not knowing where the party is." That's why we use process value analysis.

Process Value Analysis

Process value analysis focuses on classifying broader operational business processes, both in terms of their impact on strategic goals and in terms of the processes' maturity compared with those of similar companies. Relatively immature processes that have the highest impact on business strategy are the most promising candidates for improvement. In Chapter 4 we discuss a systematic approach for doing this. As with BPM maturity and value analysis, process value analysis should be repeated on a regular basis, as processes inevitably mature and change. Process value analysis also classifies processes into categories based on the type of improvements that will be made later on.

Questions process value analysis can answer:

- Which processes are most important to deliver the strategic priorities of our organization now?
- Where do our organization's processes stand in terms of relative maturity compared to competing companies that may have similar processes?
- Which processes, if improved, would have the highest impact on the business?
- What can we learn from similar processes in other industries?
- Which processes could benefit most from intervention?
- How do we classify processes into categories based on the type of improvements we intend to make later?

Creating a Roadmap to Value-Driven BPM

You create a roadmap to define which BPM capabilities to build and which processes will receive the benefit of the improved capabilities. Practitioners assign a high-level business case to each element of the roadmap so that the return on investment is clear. The roadmap to value-driven BPM unifies the process value analysis and the BPM maturity and value analysis, and begins to describe a strategy, with timelines, deliverables, and responsible parties. Over time, practitioners adjust the roadmap to address new priorities and new processes that are identified as strategically valuable. Since creating your roadmap is critical for helping you decide where BPM can provide the most value, Chapter 4 describes the creation of this roadmap in detail.

Questions a roadmap to value-driven BPM can answer:

- What required process interventions are of the highest priority?
- How can we use these to further enhance our BPM capability?
- What are the costs and benefits of the interventions?
- How can we best group these into a program of change?
- Which processes need to be improved, and in what order?
- Who will be responsible for these improvements?
- What are the milestones, performance indicators, and deliverables of the improvements?
- What's the high-level business case?

The CIO of an insurance company heard about the power of BPM and wanted to make sure that the company's BPM initiative was sustainable. The CIO appointed a vice president, and the two decided to use the Accenture BPM Capability Blueprint and the Process of Process Management as frameworks. They developed a systematic roadmap that delivered immediate benefits and established lasting capabilities. This roadmap has been executed step-by-step and revised annually. Using a Process of Process Management, the insurance company was able to make year-over-year gains, steadily moving ahead on its roadmap.

BPM Governance

BPM governance can help your organization execute on the roadmap as effectively and efficiently as possible. It includes defining roles, responsibilities, and accountabilities of members of the BPM organization, both in business and IT. It determines what combination of local or global control makes sense for the processes you are examining. Well-orchestrated collaboration among those groups is critical to the successful implementation of the PoPM. In some ways, this is the most critical piece of BPM operations—implementing proper governance helps keep all of the moving parts and people on track.

Questions BPM governance can answer:

- Who is responsible for making sure a process is working smoothly?
- How should roles and responsibilities be defined based on the PoPM?
- How are decisions made? Who makes them?
- How do we organize the decision-making process and roles?
- How should lines of business interact with IT and other enterprise support services to keep processes highly functional?
- What is the ideal set of relationships and responsibilities that will make a process efficient and provide real value to the business?

BPM governance can expose inefficiencies in a process organization even when superficially the organization is doing everything possible to keep track of processes and assign responsibility to BPM.

Here is an example: An insurance company recently tried to implement good process management across the organization. There were 23 major end-to-end processes. Each of these processes had a process owner, a process working group with representatives from every department that met monthly, and dedicated process modelers on staff. It sounds ideal—but in reality, this overly ambitious approach lost focus and didn't accomplish much. Designing a roadmap and applying BPM governance to this situation forced the company to choose four or five processes that needed this level of attention and take a less overbearing and more appropriate approach for the remaining processes.

In another example, a major financial organization decided to use a flexible process execution engine to process claims faster and more cost effectively. However, technology alone didn't help it achieve its business goals. The company had to model its processes carefully to get the promised value from the process execution system. The company put a governance organization in place to help define who can change an automated process, who needs to approve any changes, and who makes the changes happen—all of which are critical to ensuring that process automation generates its desired efficiencies, without creating unintended business disruptions.

BPM Methods and Tools

BPM methods and tools are the tactics of value-driven BPM; they comprise the ways in which improvements are actually achieved. BPM methods and tools help form an infrastructure for successful process management. Methods and tools are used to enable the value that BPM provides, encompassing the business architecture that contains all the information about the processes an organization executes, as well as related information, such as the organizational structure and the information architecture. The roadmap to value-driven BPM, developed under BPM operations, provides a schedule and guidance for aligning these methods and tools, so that they provide the most value for an organization.

Questions BPM methods and tools can answer:

* Where and how should we store process information so that it can be easily accessed, used, and reused?
* What software platforms are most appropriate for setting processes into motion?

- How should we adapt a specific process or introduce a new process to meet a certain customer need?
- Which process improvement methods can we use, and how do we do that?
- What standards and guidelines do we follow while executing BPM projects?

This component is important because many organizations start BPM initiatives by acquiring software tools, but they lack a program for effective implementation. Modeling processes is relatively easy. Setting up the models so that they are linked to real outcomes of value is very challenging, but it is key to success.

For example, a consumer goods company recently created a tremendous repository with idealized versions of nearly all its processes. But the repository was so complex and the processes bore so little resemblance to reality that it was never used. The BPM methods and tools component is there to protect organizations from such pitfalls because it connects modeling and systems activity with value outcomes—in other words, reality is kept close at hand.

Business Architecture

Business architecture contains all the information about the processes the organization executes, including related areas such as organizational structure and software architecture. Business architecture provides transparency to enable fast decisions—such as how to adapt a specific process or introduce a new process to meet a certain customer need—and the execution of the resulting actions.

Questions business architecture can answer:

- What are our processes and how are they structured?
- Where are these processes performed?
- How do these processes link to technology platforms?
- Which process supports which goals?
- What are the process KPIs?
- Which application do we use in which processes?
- Where do I use and monitor my master data?
- Who is responsible for executing a process?

BPM Standards and Guidelines

BPM standards and guidelines are instructions and procedures concerning various components of the Process of Process Management. They include standards and guidelines for using a repository, setting up the business architecture, or making a decision about process change. Artifacts of BPM standards and guidelines include modeling handbooks or procedures that define how to handle changes to process models, presentation standards, and procedures for requesting BPM support. Practitioners can also use BPM standards and guidelines to select vendors, reference models, or outsourcing partners for components of the PoPM.

Questions BPM standards and guidelines can answer:

* Which process reference models should we use?
* What are our modeling standards?
* How should we go about altering an automated process?
* Which vendors have product offerings that can help with our BPM capability and process improvement efforts?
* Which aspects of the Process of Process Management can we execute through third-party managed services?

BPM Repository

The business architecture forms the process assets of a company and is housed in a repository that enables it to be managed, used, and reused easily. The repository needs to be actively managed to remain current and useful. The repository and strategies for managing the repository are described in detail in Chapter 8.

Questions a BPM repository can answer:

* How should process models be stored and catalogued so that they can be managed, used, and reused easily?
* How can we make sure there is no overlap between our old processes and those of the company we just acquired?
* What are the use cases?

- What content should be included in the repository?
- Which formats should be used in the repository?
- How should we establish governance of the repository?
- Which tool should we use to implement the repository?

An oil and gas company acquired a new firm and needed to align the processes of the two organizations. Which processes could be used companywide, and which had to be newly defined? The company used the Accenture Reference Model as a basis for agreement on a common business architecture. It then modeled the next few layers of process. The company rolled out its newly defined processes using a process repository.

Even existing repositories can be enhanced with new dimensions. A major consumer goods company had a powerful process repository in place, created to roll out a new operating model. The problem was, it didn't effectively address risk. To mitigate operational and financial risk, the company included a risk description in its process models, as well as the related mitigation processes. It then generated its risk manual from the process repository and built risk awareness into the business architecture. This became a major component of a successful rollout of the new operating model, creating significant cost reductions with very low risk involved.

BPM Systems

BPM systems include all other technology components that will support BPM in the organization. This can include general knowledge management systems, process execution engines, rules engines, and process monitoring systems. It can also include enterprise software such as ERP and BPM-specific software such as business process management execution systems, which are discussed in more detail in Chapter 7.

Questions BPM systems can answer:

- Which hardware and software platforms support processes in the organization?

- Which vendors can support our BPM capability improvement and process improvement needs?
- How do the different software tools fit together?

Process Improvement Methods

Process improvement methods include capabilities around traditional process improvement approaches, such as Lean, TQM, and Six Sigma, but also company-specific improvement methodologies. Value-driven BPM ensures that the expertise in these approaches is available at the appropriate junctures. This expertise can be achieved through training a core team or selecting consulting partners. Chapter 5 describes how value-driven BPM harmonizes with and incorporates various process improvement techniques.

Questions process improvement methods can answer:

- How can we improve the efficiency of a given process?
- How can we eliminate waste in a workflow?
- How can we stabilize a process and make it reliable?
- How can we improve quality?

BPM Delivery

BPM delivery represents the playbook for value-driven BPM that explains how to organize tactics to get work done. BPM delivery organizes the delivery of BPM projects by describing the delivery approach for specific improvement projects, from process strategy and analysis, to design, implementation, execution, and monitoring, using the phases of the BPM life cycle (see Figure 1-1). BPM delivery defines the channel to bring the methods and tools to the organization and create the value as defined in the roadmap.

In BPM delivery, practitioners create a *process strategy*, which defines general aspects of a process, including ownership, definition of KPIs, and a framework for measuring how well it is working.

Then, through *process analysis,* practitioners apply the methods and tools to find the most significant opportunities for improvement, based on the goals developed in the roadmap.

In *process design*, practitioners establish how they will change the process in order to meet the objectives for each improvement opportunity. Next comes *process implementation,* in which the rubber hits the road, and actual changes to the processes occur. These can be purely people-oriented activities, such as changes to a workflow, purely IT-related activities, or a combination of both.

Then, once the process is implemented, BPM delivery continues through *process execution.* This can happen by using the repository for ongoing learning opportunities and teaching new people, or selectively deploying process improvement methods, each time recording the changes so that the process continuously improves and knowledge is captured.

In the *controlling and monitoring* phase, practitioners measure the KPIs that were defined at the beginning of the life cycle, and the process is monitored to ensure that the anticipated progress is being made. If progress is not happening, further adjustments can be made.

Questions BPM delivery can answer:

- How do we execute our BPM roadmap, using our methods and tools?
- How can we make sure the process change that we identify is actually implemented?
- How do we measure the process change to ensure that it meets defined performance indicators?

BPM Transformation

BPM transformation focuses on managing change and institutionalizing new ways of working so that the changes do not fade away, expanding BPM capabilities to better support larger transformation initiatives. Transformation takes a holistic approach to grouping all the related process changes aimed at delivering a single major outcome. Change programs range in scale from smaller, targeted improvements in execution excellence through to major, organization-wide transformation. Have you ever noticed a road near you dug up by the gas provider and a few months later opened up again to put in new telecommunications? Have you wondered why they couldn't better coordinate these activities? Well, transformation at a larger scale with processes also limits disruption and maximizes benefit from change.

BPM transformation is the component of value-driven BPM that supports organizational transformation efforts and establishes an overall value-driven BPM mind-set in the organization. BPM transformation uses change management tools at an organization, which consist of information, communication, and training programs for educating staff about the benefits of value-driven BPM. It also includes instructions for incorporating value-driven BPM in day-to-day activities. BPM transformation subprocesses include culture and people change management; the provision of change management, such as information, communication, and training; and program and project management—all of which are necessary to the success of large-scale change initiatives. BPM transformation also establishes a BPM community that includes process owners throughout the organization, allowing people to exchange thoughts and best practices and make value-driven BPM an integral part of their day-to-day jobs. It also sets a course for BPM project and program management.

The "people part" of value-driven BPM comes to life through BPM transformation—see Chapter 6 for a detailed look at building up a BPM organization.

Questions BPM transformation can answer:

- What are all the related process changes required to achieve a business outcome?
- What are the technical, organizational, and cultural changes that need to take place concurrently?
- How can our organization make sure that the principles of value-driven BPM actually "stick" with all the personnel in the organization?
- How can process leaders stay current and educate our people about value-driven BPM?
- How can the key lessons and takeaways from a localized improvement project be broadcast and expanded into the broader organization?
- How do I manage BPM projects to successful outcomes?

BPM Support

BPM support is the practice of embedding change in all the supporting practices, processes, and systems in your company. Underpinning all of the process areas in the Process of Process Management are key corporate, or BPM support, processes. The PoPM should engage tightly with the segments of the company that are most critical to successful and sustainable process improvements, which typically include those related to finance, procurement, human resources, and information technology. For instance, to derive maximum business value from changes made to core business processes, companies need to adjust compensation and reward systems (HR) and underlying software applications and technology (IT). One example adjustment that deeply engages BPM support might be rewarding the outcome of an overall process, not just the performance of an individual task.

With this thorough review of the Accenture Reference Model in place, we now look at common ways companies approach implementing the Process of Process Management.

DOORWAYS INTO THE PROCESS OF PROCESS MANAGEMENT

The Process of Process Management brings the components of the five major process areas together with one goal in mind: value creation. So, given that the PoPM is the central requirement for achieving value, how does your organization begin to establish its own PoPM?

As we can attest from countless client engagements, in most cases the PoPM is not established all at once, but step by step, as required by each individual organization, to achieve BPM maturity in whatever areas are necessary to meet business goals.

Establishing a Process of Process Management is not hierarchical or linear. There are any number of entry points. Figure 2-2 showed some common business situations—or trigger points—that spur organizations to implement value-driven BPM. By extension, these triggers (and many others) provide a doorway into establishing a Process of Process Management within an organization.

Here are just a few examples of the different ways that companies have started the process-centric journey, motivated by one of the common triggers, and then worked their way into establishing a more fully developed Process of Process Management.

Trigger: Postmerger Rationalization

An oil and gas company that completed a major acquisition needed to integrate the two organizations and establish standard processes to realize the intended synergies. (For more detail on this example, see Case Study 1 in Chapter 9.) The company's entry point into the Process of Process Management was via the *BPM methods and tools* section of the Reference Model.

The company began by focusing on several subprocesses within this area, such as defining common BPM standards to be used across the organization. They needed to establish a process modeling standard and then capture the high-priority "best" processes from each organization as a starting point to a common standard.

The question then became, "How do we govern all the new and improved processes?" The company turned to the *BPM operations* area of the model and its subprocesses, such as establishing a BPM Center of Excellence. Once the CoE was in place and the governance was clear, the company looked at how to build new capabilities, which led automatically to capability assessment, process value analysis, and creation of a roadmap (all aspects of BPM operations), until all of the BPM operations subprocesses had been addressed. By that point, the Process of Process Management had instantiated a strong BPM capability at the company, spanning major areas of the reference model. The company's next step is to make BPM a key component of its overall culture by addressing the capabilities in the *BPM transformation* area of the model.

Trigger: Establishment of a BPM Unit

The leadership at an investment bank saw that there were multiple small initiatives around process automation, process modeling, and process design. As a result, different business units were inventing things from scratch and using many different automation technologies to achieve their goals. The CIO concluded, "We have to set a direction and make sure we leverage our knowledge across business units." The company's entry point into the Process of Process Management was via *BPM operations.* The CIO named a manager to set up a BPM capability. His first task was to put in place a *roadmap* to value-driven BPM. To do this, he had to determine what capabilities the company already had, where to apply them, and what to do in the future. In order to execute on this roadmap, the company needed to put a *BPM governance* structure in place, and so the company continued to advance in establishing a Process of Process Management in this way.

Trigger: Innovation and Growth

A high-tech company won a large contract that required it to ramp up its engineering and production capabilities by a factor of 10 over five years. (For more detail on this example, see Case Study 2 in Chapter 9.) The head of the business unit immediately said, "Of course we have to be more efficient at everything. But the questions that keep me awake are, 'What processes do I need to change—or invest in?' and 'Do I need to invest at all?'" The issue of transparency was very important, because to make such a decision the company needed to understand its processes better.

The company's entry point into the Process of Process Management was via *BPM methods and tools*, with a goal of gaining transparency into its processes. The company established a *repository*, used a process-modeling tool, and simulated some of its key processes to identify potential bottlenecks. After focusing on this area of the reference model, the manager immediately saw that the company could stop investing in certain areas where issues were not anticipated and shift money to more valuable initiatives.

The company's leadership said, "Now we would like to roll this approach out to other business units, because this is something we really want to do in the future on a systematic basis." At that point, activity became focused on the *BPM operations* part of the model and continued from there.

In each of these cases, a company jumped in with the goal of resolving a very specific issue but then recognized the value of establishing a fuller Process of Process Management and using BPM as a management discipline.

Companies start establishing a Process of Process Management through many different doorways. The advantages and value they gain are as varied as the companies, for example:

- Standardized processes, reduced costs, and increased quality and consistency of services
- Faster integration
- Clear roles and responsibilities

- The ability to quickly implement changes that can have bottom-line impact
- Knowing how to best respond to a technology change or trend

Your BPM capability may not require all the processes shown in the Accenture Reference Model. An organization may, for example, decide not to build up capabilities regarding traditional process-improvement methods such as Six Sigma, or it may decide not to establish a formal process community, or use any process execution software, at least initially. In such cases, the related area of the Process of Process Management can be deferred. This important discussion about the scope of the BPM capability should be based on the roadmap you create, as outlined in Chapter 4.

FOUR KEY SUCCESS FACTORS FOR THE PROCESS OF PROCESS MANAGEMENT

We have found that, no matter how an organization enters the Process of Process Management, successful companies have some key characteristics in common. As companies set out to implement a Process of Process Management and implement value-driven BPM, leaders should bear in mind several representative key success factors (by no means exhaustive) that we have gleaned from research and experience.

Get Commitment from Senior Leadership

The most important factor is strong commitment from senior management, who ultimately have the responsibility for the key operational processes. As described earlier, value-driven BPM is a management discipline that should be owned and driven by management. Management would be supported by the Center of Excellence with enabling capabilities, tools, and techniques. It is critical that the initiators of any BPM strategy at a company start by engaging with senior business and IT leadership and closely align the BPM organization with business and IT strategy. Solid support and close alignment enable fast decisions during implementation and help establish BPM in the company, along with a sense of urgency. A process-centric culture begins with senior management and permeates the organization.

Score Some Quick Wins

It takes time to establish a sophisticated management discipline such as value-driven BPM. Because building the Process of Process Management often requires significant investments of effort and resources, it's helpful to build excitement and maintain interest in the big picture through some small projects that yield quick benefits. In a continuously changing business environment, you can't take years to develop BPM capabilities before benefiting from them. As described earlier, we coordinate process improvements with the development of the BPM capability itself. We recommend taking measured steps to increase your BPM capability, matched with the delivery of tangible outcomes. (See Chapter 4 for a more detailed description of this approach, which we refer to as "triangulation.") It is key to combine construction of the BPM capability with operational initiatives that deliver immediate value. In our experience, speed can be enhanced by developing and adhering to clear priorities that are focused on the business goals of an organization.

Keep It Simple

Keep things as simple as possible. The methods and tools that are available during the formation of the PoPM are a double-edged sword: they can encourage people to develop fleet and sophisticated solutions, but they can also create heavily complex and redundant processes if governance is neglected. We like to ask the question: "What is this going to be used for, by whom, to deliver what outcome?"

For instance, one company had identified more than 40 modeling methods for developing its business architecture in its repository. Not surprisingly, no businessperson used them—they were too complex and too difficult to understand. The company ultimately greatly simplified the models by using fewer than 10 methods.

In another example, at a public service organization, a dedicated team was tasked with "doing the modeling." The team worked on documenting all process areas on five levels of detail, without any real regard for how these levels would be used. This team became a small industrial enterprise in and of itself, with little business relevance.

Of course, the converse of this axiom is that a company should avoid oversimplifying things. Fostering transparency of organizational processes inherently requires a certain level of detail and sophistication, without which a company could easily create a BPM approach that looks good on paper but does not deliver the desired value.

Find the Right Degree of Freedom

Successfully implementing a Process of Process Management also requires giving people the freedom to do their jobs. Indeed, applying BPM too rigidly can make processes seem robotic and inflexible and will ultimately fail to foster the agility the company seeks. Thus, it is key to determine the degree of freedom allowed within each process. Clearly, in the case of compliance- or safety-relevant processes, such as those in finance or production, processes are often defined in detail to avoid any accidents or legal issues and, consequently, provide little freedom to do things differently. In the research and development area, however, processes may be only very roughly outlined to encourage creativity and thinking outside the box.

As you implement the Process of Process Management, you should encourage initiative and process innovation and refrain from punishing early-adopter mistakes. BPM can be used to organize process innovation by providing the right infrastructure to try out process-related ideas. This is especially important for service companies, because their offerings are also processes. The innovation of offerings can be organized through value-driven BPM and the PoPM—which means the Process of Process Management itself has to be flexible, especially in the *methods and tools* and *BPM delivery* areas.

In a great example of process innovation, emerging competition prompted a high-tech company to create a repository for greater visibility. The company, which produces compressors, started to see increasing competition from companies that it hadn't often seen in the market before. It needed a differentiator that it could implement quickly but that was not easy to copy. The company used a *BPM modeling and repository* approach to define and roll out a new delivery model, providing compressors to its clients and managing the compressors through the Internet. It started selling "compressed air" instead of compressors. The PoPM helped the company quickly identify and roll out a new, differentiating model. A well-managed BPM process is not easy to copy, so its BPM capability became another differentiator.

In summary, the Process of Process Management connects process improvements to value outcomes and establishes a management discipline around process so that each time you make an improvement to process, you don't have to reinvent the wheel. This opens the door wider for unforeseen innovations and allows improvements to happen in an organized, coordinated, and ultimately more successful way.

Note

1. Mathias Kirchmer, "The Process of Process Management: Delivering the Value of Business Process Management," Accenture, 2011.

CHAPTER 4

Developing Your Roadmap to Value-Driven BPM

When you look at all the processes at your company, it can be hard to prioritize. It may be relatively clear where to start, but what's the most important area to address next? Developing a roadmap to value-driven BPM will give you a step-by-step approach to applying BPM in areas that will provide the most value.

Based on Accenture's ongoing high-performance research and our own experience with clients, we've found that only about 15 to 20 percent of an organization's processes create deep and differentiated competitive advantage. Yes, you need all your processes to work, but which are the processes that are the most critical to delivering your brand promise? Identifying these is a critical task that allows you to pragmatically address process improvements in the right areas within the context of your current strategy and capabilities. However, it's common to be daunted by the question of which of the hundreds of business processes add the most value, or how to assess and prioritize those that most need improvement. The vital link between strategy, process, and execution should be made explicit, which is exactly what a roadmap to value-driven BPM does.

In Chapter 3, we discussed the Process of Process Management (PoPM) and noted that it is common for many organizations to enter the PoPM at the BPM operations process area. Often, the "rubber hits the road" in this area first, because it diagnoses existing processes, exposes gaps where new PoPM processes may be needed, and provides a tangible, actionable agenda for practitioners. The BPM operations area is where many organizations begin to examine existing processes for improvement potential, relate their existing processes to strategic objectives, and develop new processes. In this chapter, we discuss how your organization can identify and assess the BPM capabilities you need to develop by examining in detail several major subprocesses of BPM operations: BPM maturity and value analysis, process value analysis, and the roadmap. Through these subprocesses, the Process of Process Management comes to life in the context of your operational processes.

Developing a roadmap to value-driven BPM provides immediate benefits while building lasting capabilities. This process starts with your corporate strategy, then methodically examines the business, step by step, to create a validated roadmap for improvements. As you create the roadmap, your most important processes are identified, as are suggestions for how to improve them. By creating a roadmap to value-driven BPM, you can answer all of the following questions:

- Which processes add the most value to my business?
- Which processes are most important to focus on?
- How do I know which processes most need improvement?
- How do I assess a particular effort's improvement potential?
- In what ways might process-improvement efforts interrelate?

BEFORE YOU GET STARTED

It is no accident that the practice of BPM has suffered from an overemphasis on methods and tools and an underemphasis on business value. The simple reason is that BPM is a fascinating discipline. The prospect of defining and improving your processes is an exciting endeavor. The trick is to keep that excitement focused on creating value, not on the mechanisms of BPM. The process of developing a roadmap is one of the first areas where that excitement can take hold and get out of hand. So before we work through the detailed roadmap creation process, here are a few axioms to bear in mind on your way to achieving your goals using value-driven BPM. By keeping these principles in mind, you will be able to stay aligned with the true north of creating value.

Don't Try to Boil the Ocean

Attempting to "boil the ocean" by taking on too much—improving all processes at once—is likely to result in disappointment. An ideal roadmap is predicated on applying process improvement only to processes that are aligned with business objectives, rather than trying to apply organization-wide BPM all at once. If there is limited process-improvement capability across the organization, it is still possible to make substantial progress in BPM by strategically improving processes, improving the BPM management discipline, and capturing process knowledge in a systematic way. Having a roadmap helps to focus energy on meeting the most important business objectives and on improving the capability where it can have the most impact.

Executing the roadmap can be a multiyear enterprise, but it is unlikely to remain static throughout the time frame it describes. Ideally, you should analyze the roadmap for relevance to the current state of affairs, perhaps every few months, depending on the business environment, to determine whether you are staying on course.

Connect Strategy to Execution

The roadmap to value-driven BPM is a key tool for connecting strategy to execution. Anyone involved in BPM should be able to use the roadmap to justify his or her existence to a CEO. The answer cannot simply be, "I'm building our process repository." If you can't say why you are building the repository, you're missing the big picture.

The roadmap is designed to help you develop a direct, provable link between recognized value drivers and your work on processes. It also helps you make proper use of scarce process experts within your organization. Very few organizations have mastered this, because they are too preoccupied with individual process-improvement projects to see the strategic value of those improvements.

BPM Should Fit Your Organization

It is easy to imagine value-driven BPM as something visited upon an organization by an army of outsiders. But it shouldn't be seen this way, and it will not work if executed this way. BPM is not a stand-alone implementation by a group of experts. Implementing BPM is a critical activity that goes to the core of the organization and will result in a considerable degree of change in people, processes, and technology. Practitioners will often be faced with tough choices about when to perform small organic changes and when to initiate larger, disruptive change.

Value-driven BPM is about establishing a prioritized list of process improvements. Those priorities need to be linked to strategy and play a role in making the organization truly unique. The methods we present here can help you identify and develop your understanding of your capability to drive process improvement, but ultimately, the capability is yours. You create a roadmap to help you find the most appropriate interventions in your processes and determine which parts of the organization should lead the intervention, and when.

What's more, you can use each intervention to improve your BPM maturity and its impact on the organization. There is always room to improve both, and the improvements will be lasting, if you do both these things in unison.

The acknowledgment of the uniqueness of your organization is one of the reasons we don't dictate that the Process of Process Management be implemented fully at one time, or in a specific sequence. Instead, our aim is to show you how the universe of BPM activities interrelates but can be applied at many entry points during the BPM life cycle, depending on the particular needs of your organization.

Too Many Metrics Too Soon

Process improvement initiatives and methodologies can be overly focused on metrics. But, just as process documentation performed before the confirmation of strategic objectives can lead to disappointment, so can an overreliance on metrics as an end in themselves. In our view, in a mature environment in which process monitoring is an important part of the work, metrics are important. You need metrics and KPIs in order to gauge process performance. But an early over-investment in metrics, when you don't know what you're measuring and haven't linked the measurements to strategic value, is a premature drain on resources. As you will see in the next section, starting with a qualitative view is often more productive.

Each organization has a different and unique set of strategic priorities. It is key to link those priorities to the operating strategy. From time to time, the organization must change to react to external stimuli, and with this, priorities change. Process management needs to keep pace with this change. Awareness of strategic goals is critical to making decisions about which processes to target for improvement. In this chapter, we present tools that can help you make those decisions quickly and effectively in a dynamic environment.

Qualitative vs. Quantitative Process Analysis

Some organizations are quite mature in their process development and have created metrics that allow them to constantly keep tabs on the performance of their processes. But for many organizations beginning their practice of the management discipline of value-driven BPM, it is appropriate to start with a qualitative analysis of processes.

Often, the starting point is a conversation, the goal of which is to obtain a top-down understanding of which processes lead to which key areas of value, and then performing a qualitative assessment of improvement potential.

Another question to ask in the qualitative analysis is, "What are the key aspects of our brand, and how do they translate into processes?" In *Brand Manners: How to Create the Self-Confident Organization to Live the Brand*, Hamish Pringle and William Gordon state that "brands represent promises about what we can expect from a product, a service or a company."[1] The authors go on to define what they mean by brand manners: "Brand manners are the way in which an organization can manage its promise to customers and ensure that they are happily surprised as often as possible. These 'manners' occur in every encounter [that] takes place between the customer and the organization offering a branded product or service." In other words, it is just as relevant to consider qualitative factors such as the importance of your organization's public image as it is to look at hard numbers when analyzing the process landscape.

Once you've analyzed the question qualitatively, it is appropriate to ask, "Quantitatively, what would it mean if we improved this process at this point? Would it deliver the benefits we're looking for?"

It's important to recognize that sometimes the benefits may not be quantitatively measurable—such as customer service. The outcome may be "fuzzier" than business leaders have come to expect, but still valid and worth pursuing.

WHY YOU NEED A ROADMAP TO VALUE-DRIVEN BPM _____

With the previously mentioned principles in mind, we can now turn to the main event of this chapter: understanding why you need a roadmap and how to create one. We will start with the why.

A roadmap to value-driven BPM is vital to success because it provides a schedule of deliverables and an assignment list of responsible parties for carrying out process improvement in your organization. The roadmap provides a top-down direction for how to use process centricity to deliver more value, faster. You need a roadmap because process improvements expose complexities of your organization that are rarely dealt with in such a broad context. Your roadmap will be a very valuable asset; it tells you how you got where you are, where you should go, and how to get there. The process of creating a road-map is shown in Figure 4-1.

Roadmap Overview

The roadmap creation process begins by linking the highest-level short-term and long-term objectives to the processes that most differentiate the organization in the marketplace. Practitioners create a hierarchy of processes and subprocesses (the Logical Operating Model) so that everyone can understand in a single view the way the organization functions and the interdependencies of processes. Then, the process team begins to narrow down which processes are most critical to delivering the key value drivers. Moving on, the team conducts a capability assessment, which determines the relative maturity of these key processes, and targets those with the greatest maturity

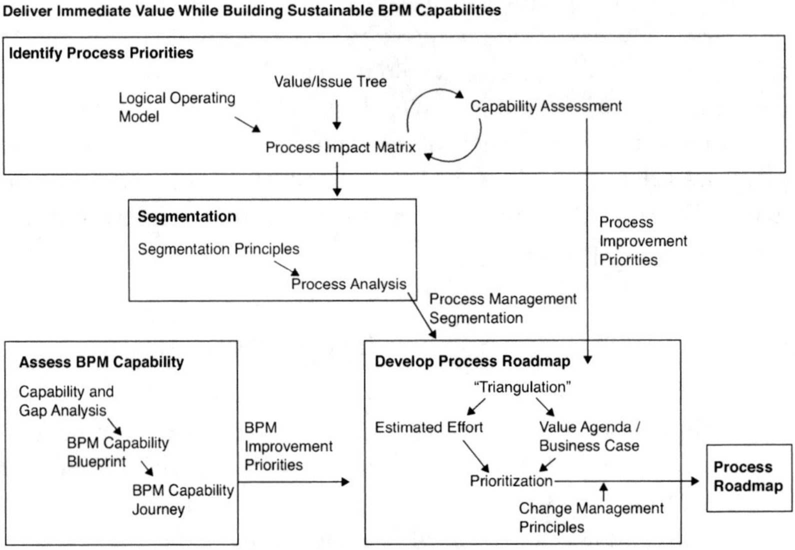

FIGURE 4-1. The Roadmap Creation Process

gaps (usually a small number) for improvement. Next, through several different lenses, the team refreshes its understanding of how routine or knowledge intensive the process is and the level of impact the process has on the organization's outside reputation or market standing. Then the team reviews the level of standardization, compared with the strategic value and relative cost of the processes, to identify major process interventions. Finally, the team assesses its own BPM maturity and improvement objectives before making the final selections and setting a schedule with deliverables, accountabilities, and concrete goals for change.

Accenture has a patent application pending for this process prioritization and roadmap creation process, as well as for the related tools and assets described in this chapter.[2]

How a Roadmap Turned a Standard ERP Implementation into a Valuable Strategic Move

ERP (enterprise resource planning) software installations can be incredibly dense undertakings that carry their own processes. Although ERP can yield great benefits to the efficiency of an organization, installing ERP is a time- and resource-intensive engagement, which is why many companies elect to outsource that effort. Many organizations see a change in ERP software as a sunk cost and simply try to reduce the expense of a version upgrade. But undertaking all of that effort, only to cement processes that are not optimized to support strategic value, is a tremendous wasted opportunity. It may actually add, rather than reduce, cost because the inefficiencies are now locked into your operations via tightly integrated software.

Often, the processes of a company that implements an ERP system begin to be dictated by the system, rather than by the company's strategic objectives. For the 80 to 85 percent of processes that are not differentiating—payroll, for example—this may be acceptable, even advantageous, because the experience of thousands of installations at a variety of clients is built into each version of software. But for the 15 to 20 percent of processes that truly make an organization stand out in its marketplace, it is a costly mistake to subjugate your organization's individuality to the complexity of a software implementation, simply because that is the cut-and-dried standard approach. Creating a roadmap to value-driven BPM can help you avoid this pitfall.

Let's take a look at how a roadmap can help in this case: An energy company had identified six strategic imperatives. At the same time, it was planning to implement SAP ERP throughout the organization. It planned to hire a low-cost outsourcing firm to handle the implementation. But then we asked, "How does this implementation connect to your six imperatives?"

The business leaders replied, "We've just got to get back to basics and get the software working."

We replied, "How are you going to implement standard processes and bring them to bear on your strategic imperatives? How does this project help you differentiate in the marketplace?"

There was no clear answer. By devising a roadmap across 270 subprocesses, we were able to identify the 80 percent of processes that did not require heavy process improvement work and could be supported with the standard software package, configured in a standard way for the energy industry. But the other 20 percent were differentiating, specialized processes keyed directly to strategic initiatives that the company had spent a great deal of time identifying. Those processes became the focus of the BPM project. It's important to identify differentiating processes clearly, as these processes can attract the bulk of the effort, while avoiding adding complexity to the remaining processes that can be dealt with using the standard method. The meticulous task of detailing processes at the transaction level for incorporation into the workflow of the software is a time and resource drain. Can your organization afford not knowing whether that work is justifiable?

ASSESS OPERATIONAL PROCESSES

Now we are ready to take a look at the roadmap creation process in more detail. Because the plan for creating value is expressed as a company's strategy, the roadmap process starts by identifying strategic priorities and matching processes to those priorities.

We'll follow the example and accompanying diagrams of a fictional oil and gas producer, Energy Inc., which recently acquired a growing company during a time of high oil prices.[3] The strategic objectives of management, postmerger, are to

- Consolidate the companies' compliance capabilities into a single unit and operational model
- Build more efficiency into contracts, project management, and operations to build resiliency for times when oil prices decline

Often a large organization has multiple views of itself, most of which are incomplete in one or more ways. It is helpful to stand back with the stakeholders and assess where the visibility gaps are, by documenting the main processes that make the organization function. The *logical operating model* diagram (Figure 4-2) outlines the basic top-level hierarchy of processes at Energy Inc. This diagram is a simplified version of an Accenture Reference Model for the energy industry called Energy Upstream. This establishes a common process language to be used across the organization.

This process view often needs to be reconciled with other views of the organization, such as the way management sees the organization of people and applications, for instance. Once you have a clear understanding of what the organization does, the next step is to look at the goals of the company against the differentiating value drivers.

The *Issue Tree* is used to translate business priorities into strategic objectives and to relate them to value drivers. For example, as shown in Figure 4-3, at Energy Inc., the high-level business priority of establishing itself as a "leader in safety and environmental performance" meant that the safety of personnel and contractors had to be a strategic objective. The best approaches to achieving that objective

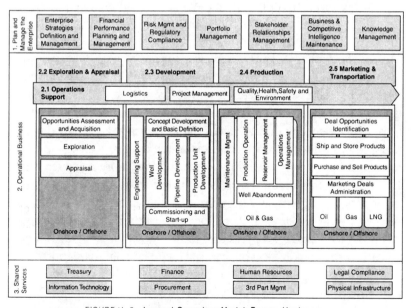

FIGURE 4-2. Logical Operating Model: Energy Upstream

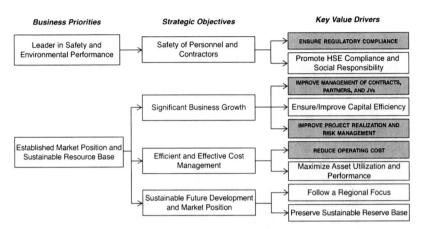

FIGURE 4-3. Sample Issue Tree for Energy Inc.

were the key value drivers of ensuring regulatory compliance at the top level and promoting health, safety, and environmental (HSE) compliance and social responsibility at the next level. Simply put, the organization needed to ensure safety and compliance in a time of heightened political and social awareness about the practice of petroleum extraction and refining. At the same time, the company wanted to use the improved cash flow that was the result of a relatively high oil price to make itself more resilient to future market changes.

Once the key drivers are narrowed down (highlighted in bold on the Issue Tree), the next step is to place them in the *Process Impact Matrix* (Figure 4-4). In the Process Impact Matrix, processes are ranked according to their impact on key value drivers. The object is to take the main value drivers from the Issue Tree and place these in the center columns of the Process Impact Matrix. Processes are listed in rows. Depending on the level of analytic rigor an organization is prepared to undertake, the columns of the matrix can be populated using a simple survey technique or with much more analytical rigor. Examples of this include process cost analysis, complexity assessment, risk assessment, and prime value-chain analysis. The ideal type of analysis varies for each value driver, and there may be reference examples available for a particular industry, which give practitioners a head start. The key is to have as balanced an analysis as possible.

For example, in a recent engagement, we at first had only operational personnel in a room to review the Process Impact Matrix, and the various planning processes were deemed to be unimportant.

#	Level 1	Level 2	Level 3	Ensure Regulatory Compliance 35.0%	Improve Management of Contracts, Partners, and JVs 10.0%	Improve Project Realization and Risk Management 20.0%	Reduce Operating Cost 35.0%	Average Score 100%	RED
31	Operational Business-Development	Well Development	Development Drilling & Completion	1	1	3	3	2.1	2
32	Operational Business-Development	Well Development	Development Field Operational Plan	1	2	3	3	2.2	2
33	Operational Business-Development	Well Development	Commissioning & Start-up	1	1	3	1	1.4	1
34	Operational Business-Production	Production Operations	Produce the Field	3	2	2	3	2.7	2
35	Operational Business-Production	Production Operations	Identify and Develop Further Opportunities	1	2	2	2	1.7	0
36	Operational Business-Production	Reservoir Management	Reservoir Management	1	1	3	3	2.1	2
37	Operational Business-Production	Production Operations	Oil & Gas Sales	1	3	1	1	1.2	1
38	Operational Business-Production	Well Abandonment	Abandon Assets	1	2	1	2	1.4	0
39	Operational Business-Production	Operations Management	Project Management	1	2	3	3	2.2	2
40	Operational Business-Production	Operations Management	Research & Development	1	1	1	1	1.0	0
41	Shared Services	Physical Infrastructure	Property/Facility Management	1	1	1	1	1.0	0

FIGURE 4-4. Extract of Process Impact Matrix for Energy Inc.

#	Level 3 Process	Performance		Assessment			
		Current	Ideal	Basic	Advanced	Leading	Emerging
3	Corporate QHSE	2.5	2.6		ΔΔ		
17	Acquire Asset(s)	3.1	3.5			Δ ▲	▲
18	Manage Exploration Work Program	1.1	3.6	Δ			▲
20	Generate and Identify Drilling Targets	1.5	3.7	Δ			▲
21	Exploration Drilling	1.6	3.2	Δ		▲	
23	Manage Appraisal Work Program	1.2	2.8	Δ		▲	
25	Define Technical Development Concepts	2.2	3.3		Δ	▲	
28	Field Development Plan	1.1	2.6	Δ	▲		
29	Final Drilling Planning	3.3	3.4			ΔΔ	
30	Design and Construct Surface Facilities	2.1	2.8		Δ ▲		
31	Development Drilling and Completion	3.1	3.2			ΔΔ	
32	Develop Field Operational Plan	1.2	3.9	Δ			▲
34	Produce the Field	2.3	3.8		Δ		▲
36	Reservoir Management	2.2	2.6		Δ ▲		
39	Project Management	1.3	3.5	Δ			▲
56	Source to Contract	2.8	2.9			ΔΔ	

FIGURE 4-5 Capability Assessment Results for Energy Inc.

"There is no value from the head office," they stated. With more work, we found that not only were the planning processes quite important but that they actually required the most work for improvement. It is therefore critical to have the right balance of input into the process.

Energy Inc. started with 165 processes. Each process is evaluated for its impact on each key value driver—1 being highest, 3 being lowest. Eventually, Energy Inc. narrowed the list down to 16 high-priority processes.

This exercise is important because it establishes a clear understanding of value drivers and their links to processes. Let's face it: every department feels its own processes are the most critical. This is where the need for quantitative evaluation arises—assigning numbers and ranking processes forces a discussion about what's really important.

That said, quantitative rankings can be informed by any kind of information deemed appropriate—which could be quantitative (such as cost or return on invested capital) or qualitative (relevance to strategic objectives). The act of assigning some kind of numerical value helps to make the conversation more specific and ranks options so that decisions can be made.

We now want to assess the maturity of each of the 16 high-impact processes identified in the Process Impact Matrix. We do this by referring to the *Capability Assessment Model* for each process and rating the processes at one of four stages of maturity. The results of this assessment are shown in Figure 4-5. Here, the current and desired states of maturity are shown for each process, and it's easy to see where the biggest gaps are.

There are various methods for qualitatively assessing the maturity of processes. Companies such as Accenture have reference Capability Assessment Models for all major processes that can be used for this purpose.

In our current example, we highlight the 16 processes Energy Inc. identified in the Process Impact Matrix. One of four states of maturity is assigned to each process—basic, advanced, leading, and emerging—across three different areas—process, people, and technology. Using surveys, stakeholders in the organization are asked to map where they think each process is in terms of its maturity, and where they think it should be to serve strategic objectives. In this instance, the 10 processes with the broadest gaps between basic and emerging are highlighted and selected to move further on through the roadmap process.

The relatively simple practice of ranking and prioritizing processes can break a seemingly overwhelming task into manageable pieces, and, importantly, give management the confidence that the processes being targeted are most likely to provide more value if improved. The capability assessment (shown in Figure 4-5) provides a good basis for a more detailed management workshop to develop a deeper understanding of these capability gaps. As mentioned earlier, a wide range of analytical techniques can be used to bring deeper and more quantitative facts into this discussion.

QUANTIFY WHAT INTERVENTIONS MIGHT LOOK LIKE _____

Having settled on a limited number of processes to target for improvement, we now decide how to close the gaps revealed by the assessment, undertaking specific actions to foster process improvements that can be tied to a specific outcome of value.

Segmentation

We now want to establish what kind of intervention is best suited to closing the capability gaps identified earlier and determine who should drive this effort. An intervention is simply a way to understand

and improve the design and implementation of a process. To help us understand what an intervention might look like, we segment and classify processes. In this stage, we evaluate the strategic importance of the processes selected for further evaluation and the amount of standardization required by the processes.

Strategic Importance

Energy Inc. began this stage by looking at the processes' strategic value. This is different from the assessment done earlier (which connected processes to current value drivers); the issue here is long-term business intent and a process's role in helping the company reach that goal.

Strategic importance refers to any process that requires a high degree of knowledge intensity and has a high customer impact. These processes are important to an organization's long-term business strategy. As a caveat, we don't mean to say here that any one process is unimportant. But many processes are somewhat routine and transactional in nature and exist in the background, as far as the customer is concerned.

Knowledge Intensity vs. Customer Impact

To understand the strategic importance of a process, we investigate the relationship of a process to the long-term business intentions of the company and evaluate the process's role in helping the company achieve that goal. The Knowledge Intensity vs. Customer Impact graphic (Figure 4-6) shows a group of bubbles in a field above the junction of the x and y axes. Each bubble represents a process, and each bears its original number from when it was part of the list of 163 processes at the beginning of the assessment. For example, line 34 in the Capability Assessment Results (Figure 4-5), "Produce the Field," becomes bubble 34 in the Knowledge Intensity vs. Customer Impact diagram.

Knowledge Intensity: This variable (on the x-axis) speaks to a process's depth and complexity. Is it a low-end process? One example is a process that is purely transactional, such as paying suppliers. Or is it high-end—a process that requires experience and complex decision making? Processes with high knowledge intensity are often associated with competitive advantage because they are potentially unique to the company and hard for competitors to duplicate. These

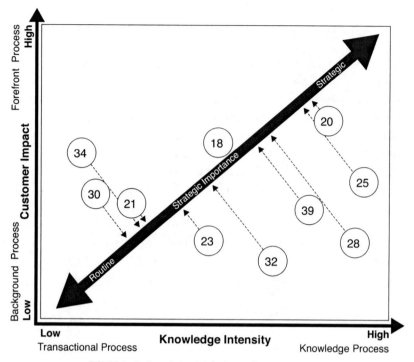

FIGURE 4-6. Knowledge Intensity vs. Customer Impact

processes are seldom predictable and need deep insight to execute. Pricing, planning, forecasting, research, and new product development are good examples.

Customer Impact: This variable (the *y*-axis) is the degree to which a process influences the customer experience or the external impression of the company. A process that is high on the customer impact scale is not necessarily visible to the customer, but it affects the company's relationship with the customer. For example, a particular process may be critical if merchandising is a top concern. Another might be key if superior support is a strategic cornerstone. A third process might be important if customers are most concerned about low purchase cost. Put another way, processes associated with higher customer impact are likely those that are critical to your brand. Lower on the scale are those that are important to the organization, but not directly germane to the customer's relationship with the company.

Figure 4-6 shows that the high–knowledge intensity, high-impact processes occupy the upper right quadrant, while "low-low" processes fall at the bottom left. The upper-rightmost processes are those with the highest strategic importance. At this point, the same Energy Inc. stakeholders who completed the capability assessment were interviewed again about the 10 priority processes highlighted in the assessment. These stakeholders were asked to rate each of the processes in the two areas "knowledge intensity" and "customer impact." The same set of interviews is used to rate another area, "standardization," described later in this chapter.

Figure 4-6 shows the net result of this process. Energy Inc. was able to determine that, among the 10 processes, Generate and Identify Drilling Targets (20) and Define Technical Development Concepts (25) were the processes with the most strategic importance, while Design and Construct Surface Facilities (30) and Produce the Field (34) have the least strategic importance.

Process Management Assessment

The Process Management Assessment helps highlight which intervention approach may be optimal and informs governance needed around that technique.

To conduct this assessment, the entire graph is rotated counterclockwise 45 degrees, so that the strategic importance line is now the y-axis (Figure 4-7). A new x-axis is created: standardization. The data for this variable are created from the same set of interviews described earlier, which surveyed stakeholders about the degree to which a process is (or should be) standardized. As a dimension of standardization, should the process have centralized or local control? The bubbles representing each process are now arranged according to this factor.

The final assessment dimension, after strategic value and standardization, examines the cost of the process. This is demonstrated by the relative size of the bubbles—for example, bubble 34, Produce the Field, would be the highest cost to improve and the least strategic of the 10 processes selected for analysis.

To draw some conclusions from this assessment, we highlight the four quadrants shown in Figure 4-7.

Processes in the upper right quadrant are strategically important and will benefit from strong central management. The lower right quadrant indicates that a process is more routine but, again, could

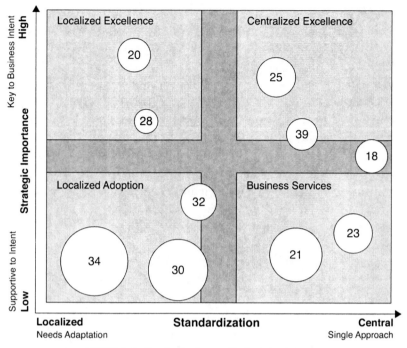

FIGURE 4-7. Standardization vs. Strategic Importance

benefit from strong central control. The lower left quadrant is routine but can benefit from local control. The upper left quadrant is more strategic but nonetheless needs local control.

In between the quadrants is a gray "parking lot" for processes that do not fall directly into one of the quadrants; it is not always crystal clear how to prioritize these processes. Processes that fall into the parking lot need more analysis and discussion.

Placing processes in each quadrant has a particular meaning. Let's take a quick look at each of the quadrants.

Centralized Excellence (Top Right) Centralized Excellence describes processes that deliver the best value when managed centrally. These usually include processes like product development, pricing, and the management of large customer relationships. The process owner for these processes should be at a global level. The governance for these processes requires a fairly high-touch, customized approach—the classic case of "massaging the big accounts." It's also important to place a lot of emphasis on innovation for processes in this quadrant, because doing so will yield the most benefit. This is a poor area to apply a pure process-improvement technique such as Six Sigma, which focuses on eliminating variance—in fact, this is where you want innovation and some variance to shine.

For example, Define Technical Development Concepts (25) is a process that Energy Inc. has determined is worth upgrading. The company can discern from the process's position in the upper right quadrant that the activity is largely centralized and of high strategic importance. We can conclude that improvements should emphasize managing process change and execution in a way that applies uniformly across the organization and ensures that strong levels of innovation are applied (consistent with the strategic nature of the process).

Localized Excellence (Top Left) Localized Excellence denotes processes that deliver the best value when administered locally or that are based on an explicit understanding of local customs or business practices. These typically include processes like local supply chains and customer relations. For Energy Inc., this includes processes such as Generate and Identify Drilling Targets (20) and Field Development Plan (28). In this company's case, an understanding of local geology, hydrology, politics, and property boundaries would be key to a successful drilling location campaign. As was once said in *The Music Man,* "You gotta know the territory." A local manager would be the process owner, borrowing from company-wide best practices, with an open line to central management for the occasional high-touch account scenario, but with plenty of leeway for localized customization and innovation.

Business Services (Lower Right) Business Services typically include finance, accounting, and application support. These necessary but less strategic functions are best managed by a central authority and provide more value as they are more standardized. Very few companies differentiate on accounts payable—unless they are notoriously slow or make a lot of mistakes. For some companies, these processes are good candidates for outsourcing, automation, or the application of Six Sigma or other process-improvement techniques.

For example, Exploration Drilling (21) is the practice of drilling sample cores all over the countryside to test the geology and hydrology of a potential drilling location. At Energy Inc., this is a centralized, somewhat routine, and quite cost-intensive process. An initial assessment might make this process a good candidate for increasing compliance to reduce risk and potentially outsourcing, to drive greater efficiency and reduce cost.

Localized Adoption (Lower Left) In this quadrant we place processes that are localized and fairly routine in terms of strategic importance. These would typically include processes like customs clearance, local taxes, and those related to human resources. Here, it makes sense to look to the local geographic or industry standard for process excellence, with minor adaptations to fit your organization. A process in the bottom left quadrant—say, Energy Inc.'s Produce the Field process (34)—focuses primarily on production at a specific location. It is highly repetitive, with significant costs. Improvement efforts may need to focus on enhancements that are largely transactional but nonetheless require customization for each instance. Compliance, applications of Six Sigma, and efforts aimed at increasing cost efficiency could be most viable. Software that has many of these practices built in may also be valuable here.

Not Sure Where to Put It? Use the "Parking Lot" In any large organization, this matrix is likely to promote a lively and important management conversation that strikes at the core mission of the company. Different members of management will respond in different ways about the same processes. Some processes may fall into more than one quadrant initially. For example, a global process owner could drive consistency, quality, pricing, and standard product definition. A local representative could drive relationship, service, and localized pricing. When you can see the case for both local and global ownership, it's hard to decide which quadrant the process should reside in.

When there is not enough information to determine which quadrant the process belongs in, these ambiguous or multiquadrant processes are quarantined for further discussion in the "parking lot" of the gray area between the quadrants of Figure 4-7. An example of a "parking lot process" at Energy Inc. is Manage Exploration Work Program (18), which is a small bubble at center right. This process keeps central oversight of all drilling projects. It allocates resources and monitors progress. This is a low-cost but strategically valuable process that is highly centralized, and it could return a high bang for the buck. This process sits right at the top end of the quadrant, and it has a number of routine elements, but it also needs good experience to effectively balance resource allocation. This is a key, differentiating capability, kept in-house but run as a global shared service. Further analysis showed this process to be in need of much more robust planning and analytic skills and that it could be executed much more centrally.

It is often possible, and necessary, to split key processes into parts when they do not fit into a specific quadrant. As you do this, the organization of your firm becomes clear in a granular way that is quite rare. This exercise of associating value with each process, and understanding dependencies between processes, regions, and business lines, is hugely valuable. It prevents the kind of "boil the ocean" mistakes described earlier in the chapter. Driving a process globally is not always the right thing to do—nor is buying a huge ERP upgrade every few years and simply trying to squeeze all the cost out of it, without looking at how your processes track to value and how changes in your processes affect your management and organization.

IDENTIFY THE APPROPRIATE BPM CAPABILITIES

Once you have identified key processes to improve, it is time to step back and take stock of your BPM capabilities and gauge your maturity in all of the factors that affect process quality.

Much of the work of BPM is rooted in, lives in, and starts in other parts of the organization, including infrastructure, policies, and standards. BPM should be deep within a firm's culture. Assessing BPM capability means looking at the interrelation of all these factors, which can be seen in the BPM Capability Blueprint (as shown in Figure 1-2).

Now is the time to conduct a capability assessment of the Process of Process Management (see Chapter 3). This is also a good point to use the Capability Assessment Model. Now, instead of evaluating the maturity of individual processes, you evaluate the maturity of your BPM capability. The key is to match your capability and maturity to move the agenda forward, with an attainable benefit attached.

TRIANGULATE

As described in Chapter 1, sustainable value is achieved when you have a balanced focus on execution excellence and the supporting BPM discipline. As you navigate your BPM journey, you will begin to notice places where you can "triangulate" your efforts—when improving one process in a single project, you can also improve your BPM capabilities at the same time by capturing your activity as a suggested best practice, or even capturing "next time, try it this way" information.

To triangulate, first ask, "What is the operational business need?" Then, "What are the strengths of the organization in terms of BPM capability?" When these two questions are brought together, the third leg of the triangle is created—the individual process initiatives.

For example, the "capability" leg could be represented by a strong Six Sigma capability at the organization. The "operational business need" could be a large, costly process that needs to be rationalized. The third "process initiative" leg—the action taken—would be to use Six Sigma to rationalize the costly process. Figure 4-8 illustrates the triangulation process.

Triangulation is different from simply improving the processes you already have. Process improvement methods are typically about

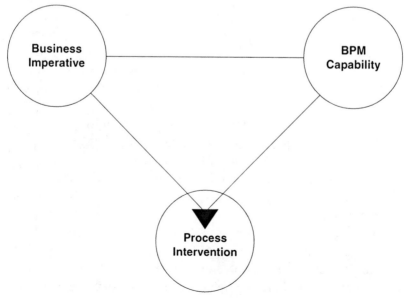

FIGURE 4-8. Triangulation

optimizing existing processes, but not necessarily about building new and better processes where there is weakness. For example, Six Sigma is an effective process improvement technique for eliminating variance from a process. A simple triangulation would be to apply Six Sigma to a high-cost process that is well documented and optimized but could go faster. But Six Sigma would not be the optimal choice for redesigning a process.

A more challenging but more valuable intervention would be to build a new capability in an area where your organization is not as strong—say, its product development—improving the process along the way and adding new processes, as you bring on new hires, add and improve modeling software and market testing, and so on. That's triangulation.

In the Energy Inc. example, there are two strong examples of triangulation. In the first example, the team concluded that there was a need for greater standardization of the field operational processes (process intervention) in order to improve compliance (business imperative) and get the benefit of improved project planning. Energy Inc. used this opportunity to establish a centralized repository of business processes (BPM capability improvement) as a way of certifying agreement on the standard processes and driving compliance.

In the second example, once these operational processes had been documented, the newly formed BPM team applied simulation techniques to better understand what was driving the efficiency. The availability of site-based resources was identified as the key shortcoming that led to downtime at the company. This was fixed by driving innovation into the planning process. This is also a triangulation that led to improved operational performance *and* enhanced BPM capabilities.

The triangulation concept recognizes that decisions are often made in the heat of battle—no one sets out to conduct process improvement in a vacuum. Similarly, no one conducts a process simulation unless there is a reason to improve that process. But whenever the intervention works, the entire procedure that leads up to that intervention can be captured as a best practice, so that the next time you need to intervene in a process, you will have an improved process for doing so.

We will cover the relationship of value-driven BPM to process improvement techniques, modeling, storage, and deployment of best practices in Chapter 5.

CREATE A ROADMAP

Now you have assessed your BPM capabilities and made an honest assessment of the strategic value of your processes. Each project selected for the roadmap will need to show good results from triangulation, have a high-level business case, and have an achievable timeline. You have selected the processes that need improvement and have used triangulation to identify potential intervention initiatives. Now, normal project management practices can kick in.

As with any project, you need to assess the effort that will be required to implement the interventions and estimate the scale of benefit that could be achieved. Normal practice would then evaluate whether the initiative is justified, then group related activities together into logical projects.

Placing the initiatives onto a 2 × 2 Effort vs. Benefit matrix that maps effort (and complexity) against value (strategic value, not just bottom-line impact) is a useful technique that can make the trade-offs more visible and easier to understand. This allows you to distill one more level of certainty about which processes to target. "Effort" can be summed up as "time, money, and resources." "Benefit" encapsulates all of the strategic value we have described previously, both qualitative and quantitative. Those interventions that meet nearest the upper right corner are the most likely to reward your efforts.

THE FINAL RESULT: YOUR ROADMAP TO VALUE-DRIVEN BPM

The final product, the roadmap to value-driven BPM, is very simply a schedule, showing specific steps to be taken at specific milestones, by specific people or organizational units, and assigning responsibility for them. Ideally, it is not etched in stone—the schedule should be updated to reflect changing circumstances. But the structure of accountability and the links between process, people, and time should remain intact. Your roadmap is itself a triangulation—it improves your operational processes and your BPM capabilities at once. It allows you to clearly understand dependencies between improvements, their strategic value, and their organizational effects. It charts a path to lasting benefits.

Notes

1. Hamish Pringle and William Gordon, *Brand Manners: How to Create the Self-Confident Organization to Live the Brand* (Chichester, UK: John Wiley & Sons, 2001).

2. Peter Franz, "Prioritizing Process Improvements to Maximize Business Agility," Accenture, 2011.

3. This example of the hypothetical oil and gas company, Energy Inc., is presented in Peter Franz, "Prioritizing Process Improvements to Maximize Business Agility," Accenture, 2011.

CHAPTER 5

How Value-Driven BPM Optimizes the Impact of Process Improvement Initiatives

On your journey to execution excellence, you may have built expertise in any number of process improvement initiatives, such as Lean, Six Sigma, TQM, and others. This chapter explains how you can use value-driven BPM to ensure the right focus with those capabilities to drive the most sustainable business value.

The first four chapters of this book explained how value-driven BPM represents an evolution of BPM from a set of tactical methods focused on improving processes in isolation into a management discipline that touches all of the processes at an organization. We demonstrated how to close the gap between BPM as a set of tactical methods and BPM as a management discipline.

Now, we address a question that often arises in our work: "What is the relationship between value-driven BPM and what's traditionally been thought of as process improvement?" Value-driven BPM is a structured and pragmatic approach that helps you build on all of the progress that has been made in process improvement and BPM up until now—it organizes the loose agglomeration of methods and tools that has collectively come to be known as process management, process improvement, or BPM. Value-driven BPM rationalizes all these "bits and parts" into a cohesive whole, imbeds it in the organization's culture, and, critically, attaches BPM activities to outcomes of value—results that people want.

VALUE-DRIVEN BPM AND PROCESS IMPROVEMENT METHODS

When many people think of BPM, process improvement techniques such as Six Sigma, Total Quality Management, Lean, or process automation come to mind. These techniques have, for the most part, driven significant business value and have collectively advanced the management practice of BPM. While it incorporates these techniques, value-driven BPM is distinct from them and operates on a wider playing field. Given the prevalence of these methods in the current practice of management, it's important that we carefully delineate the boundaries between what it means to practice value-driven BPM and what it means to execute a process improvement program using these methods.

Value-driven BPM is not contradictory or oppositional to any of these process improvement initiatives. In fact, as demonstrated in Chapters 3 and 4, through the Process of Process Management value-driven BPM devotes an entire area, BPM methods and tools, to appropriately applying process improvement initiatives. But it would also be a mistake to presume that any of these methods always has the same ambition and scope as value-driven BPM.

What makes value-driven BPM distinct? Value-driven BPM is a management discipline. As we explained in Chapters 1 and 2, value-driven BPM is an overarching approach that attempts to use value as an organizing principle, offering a systematic way of evaluating what's important and what is not important about the way a business is run, then using various practices of BPM to methodically improve that business. Value-driven BPM makes a declaration that the Process of Process Management is so fundamental that it should be practiced in *every* aspect of a business, the same way other management disciplines are.

Process improvement initiatives allow you to examine a process and make it more effective. But they don't necessarily help you determine which processes should be examined in the first place. Value-driven BPM helps you determine which processes are most important and which improvements would make your business run the best. As we demonstrated in Chapter 4, the roadmap creation process is a methodical approach for selecting and improving targeted processes and the overall BPM capability simultaneously.

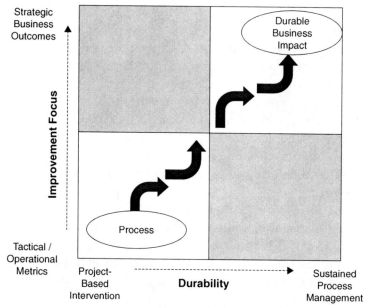

FIGURE 5-1. Focus of Value-Driven BPM: Durable Business Impact

Given the preponderance of enthusiastic practitioners of process improvement methods, we as proponents of value-driven BPM frequently find ourselves explaining that value-driven BPM is neither synonymous with nor duplicative of Six Sigma, Lean, or Total Quality Management. In some ways, this chapter repeats and reiterates the conversation that we have had at multiple organizations all over the world, confirming our assertion that value-driven BPM is operating at a higher level and is inclusive of these methods.

Value-driven BPM is the concurrent attention to process improvement initiatives and the organizational discipline to realize the improvement value and to sustain this over time. As illustrated in Figure 5-1, the level of business impact increases when you properly focus any intervention on business outcomes and build durable governance and oversight into the normal working culture of the organization.

Value-driven BPM is thus easily harmonized with all these process improvement methods, because once you have assigned the right strategic priority to a process that needs improvement, you can then decide to improve that process using any of these methods.

Value-driven BPM will help you decide which of these process improvement methods to use.

A second goal of this chapter is to explain the personality (primary characteristics and usage context) of each of these process improvement methods so that, as a value-driven BPM practitioner, you can understand how and when to apply them. Value-driven BPM also helps to decide when to make large leaps forward (business transformation) and when to conduct incremental improvements (as, for example, advocated by *Kaizen*). It then further plays a very important role in deciding where and how to focus transformations or improvements.

Table 5-1 provides an overview of some of the major standard process improvement methods and their use cases. We have purposely used general definitions as an illustration of where their prime focus is. There are many other examples of these techniques where they have been extended to cover some of the value orientation embodied in BPM.

TABLE 5-1. Process Improvement Methods

Method	Description	Use Condition
Lean	Considers the expenditure of resources for any goal other than the creation of value for the end customer to be wasteful, and thus a target for elimination. Working from the perspective of the customer who consumes a product or service, "value" is defined as any action or process for which a customer would be willing to pay.[1] It also enables process and enterprise speed.	"It costs too much and takes too long."
Six Sigma	Six Sigma seeks to improve the quality of process outputs by identifying and removing the causes of defects (errors) and minimizing variability in manufacturing and business processes. It uses a set of quality management methods, including statistical methods, and creates a special infrastructure of people within the organization ("Black Belts," "Green Belts," etc.) who are experts in these methods. Each Six Sigma project carried out within an organization follows a defined sequence of steps and has quantified financial targets (cost reduction or profit increase).[2]	"The results are too variable."
Lean Six Sigma	The combination of Lean and Six Sigma.[3]	"The results are too variable and the process costs too much."

TABLE 5-1. Process Improvement Methods, *continued*

Method	Description	Use Condition
DMAIC	Used for projects aimed at improving an existing business process, DMAIC includes these steps: Define the problem. Measure key aspects of the current process and reflect relevant data. Analyze the data to investigate and verify cause-and-effect relationships. Improve or optimize the existing process. Set up pilot runs to establish process capability. Control the future state process to ensure that any deviations from target are corrected before resulting in defects.[4]	"We need a systematic way to improve this process."
DMADV	Used for generating new business processes, DMADV follows these steps: Define design goals that are consistent with customer demands and the enterprise strategy. Measure and identify CTQs (characteristics that are Critical To Quality), product capabilities, production process capability, and risks. Analyze to develop and design alternatives, create a high-level design, and evaluate design capability to select the best design. Design details, optimize the design, and plan for design verification. This phase may require simulations. Verify the design, set up pilot runs, implement the production process, and hand it over to the process owner(s).[5]	"We need a new business process."
DFSS	DFSS is design for Six Sigma (considered to be synonymous with DMADV).[6]	"We need a new business process."
TQM	Total Quality Management is a continuous improvement methodology with nine common practices: Cross-functional process design Process management Supplier quality management Customer involvement Information and feedback Committed leadership Strategic planning Cross-functional training Employee involvement[7]	"The quality is unacceptable."

(continued)

TABLE 5-1. Process Improvement Methods, *continued*

Method	Description	Use Condition
QFD	Quality Function Deployment is a method to transform user demands into design quality, to deploy the functions forming quality, and to deploy methods for achieving the design quality into subsystems and component parts, and ultimately to specific elements of the manufacturing process.[8]	"We need an explicit way to connect user demand to specific improvements."
Kaizen	Japanese for "improvement" or "change for the better," *Kaizen* refers to a philosophy or practices that focus on continuous improvement of processes. Emphasis is on teamwork, involving all employees, and using the scientific method to pinpoint improvement opportunities and eliminate waste.[9]	"We need better staff cohesion around process goals."

1. John F. Krafcik, "Triumph of the Lean Production System," *Sloan Management Review*, 30, no. 1 (Fall 1988): 41–52.
2. Mikel Harry and Richard Schroeder, *Six Sigma* (New York: Random House, 2000).
3. Mark O. George, *The Lean Six Sigma Guide to Doing More with Less* (Hoboken, NJ: John Wiley & Sons, 2010).
4. Joseph DeFeo and William Barnard, *Juran Institute's Six Sigma Breakthrough and Beyond: Quality Performance Breakthrough Methods* (New York: McGraw-Hill, 2004).
5. W. Edwards Deming, "Out of the Crisis," MIT Center for Advanced Engineering Study, 1986.
6. Subir Chowdhury, *Design for Six Sigma* (Chicago: Dearborn Trade, 2002).
7. Kristy O. Cua, Kathleen E. McKone, and Roger G. Schroeder, "Relationships Between Implementation of TQM, JIT, and TPM and Manufacturing Performance," *Journal of Operations Management*, 19 (2001): 675–694.
8. Joseph P. Ficalora and Lou Cohen, *Quality Function Deployment & Six Sigma*, 2nd ed. (Upper Saddle River, NJ: Prentice Hall, 2009).
9. Masaaki Imai, Kaizen: *The Key to Japan's Competitive Success* (New York: Random House, 1986).

This chapter is organized around the intersection of four basic classes of process improvement methods, all of which can be better coordinated, and better connected to value outcomes, through the application of value-driven BPM.

FOUR CLASSES OF PROCESS IMPROVEMENT METHODS APPLIED THROUGH VALUE-DRIVEN BPM

To use these process improvement methods in harmony with value-driven BPM, it's important to understand two things: the personality of each process improvement method and the way that value-driven BPM helps to improve its implementation.

We have categorized process improvement approaches in terms of their point of origin and, broadly speaking, whether their solutions are primarily organizational (people-based) or technological (IT-based). If you think of these four classes as an organizing principle, you will better understand which of these process improvement methods to apply at any one time in any given situation.

- *Top-down:* These initiatives are typically orchestrated from a central point of control by senior management and have organization-spanning implications, targeted at end-to-end processes or major parts of the business.
- *Bottom-up:* These initiatives are typically tactical approaches to improving individual processes and departmental workflows, or subprocesses in smaller parts of the organization.
- *People-centric:* These are initiatives where the principal change is to the activities and workflows in an organization.
- *IT-centric:* These initiatives largely consist of automation.

In practice, these approaches are often combined. Table 5-2 illustrates some example classifications of process improvement initiatives.

TABLE 5-2. Example Classifications of Basic Process Improvement Initiatives

Approach Examples	People-centric	IT-centric
Top-down	Business process transformation, "classic" reengineering	Enterprise resource planning (ERP) implementation or optimization
Bottom-up	*Kaizen*, Lean, Six Sigma, Total Quality Management	Business process management system (BPMS), departmental workflow

Now that we understand the classes, we can briefly review each one and discuss how value-driven BPM helps practitioners select the right approach and use it to its greatest effect.

BUSINESS PROCESS TRANSFORMATION (TOP-DOWN, PEOPLE-CENTRIC)

When approaching a situation in which a business process transformation is being used, it is important to not only redesign and redefine processes but also to consider all of the related processes and the perceived gains involved. Value-driven BPM helps identify those processes that could benefit from interventions (as described in Chapter 4) and ensures that the end-to-end impact of any change is well understood. The Process of Process Management provides a context that keeps these initiatives strategically focused, as they have organization-spanning implications. In order to effectively perpetuate change, business process transformation under the guise of value-driven BPM also means corralling the engagement of BPM support functions, such as the HR, finance, and legal departments, which also span the organization.

Point Business Process Transformation at the Right Target

Think of business process transformation or any ambitious process improvement approach as a laser that can zero in on known issues with existing processes and eliminate the inconsistencies and trouble spots that have prevented processes from working as they should. This laser has been very effective in the past, but it needs to be applied where it can have the most benefit and payoff.

The focus of value-driven BPM is on the most strategic parts of the business, with two primary goals: focusing resources on the right processes and getting things done to produce real results. When organizations set out to make changes, often the change initiators find themselves stuck doing blanket "as-is" and "to-be" corrections across the organization. The effort is appreciated, but the end result is a group of aspirational documents and very little real change. Value-driven BPM helps to focus such efforts on the right processes—where it counts—and clearly charts the path of how to get there and produce real results.

Pointing Transformation at the Right Targets at a Chemical Company

A transformation program at a chemical company provides a strong example of how value-driven BPM can properly focus and prioritize efforts to change. The plant manager of the company was concerned about minimizing labor costs. Almost every transformation program at the plant focused on that aim. Many different approaches and methods were applied, from increased automation to business process outsourcing. Despite these efforts, the plant's financial performance was above average but not in the top quartile. After evaluating the situation using value-driven BPM, leadership discovered that the plant was extremely inefficient in its energy usage. Reducing labor costs had become an obsession, obscuring other opportunities for improvement. One of the largest benefits of value-driven BPM is its ability to break through biases and preconceptions and highlight areas that can produce the most results.

Proper Scoping of Business Transformation

One of the critical failure points of business transformation programs is that practitioners set out with too modest a scope. Business transformation is a major change to the organization. It is more than just tweaking a process. Too often, business transformation shrinks, for a variety of reasons, into a small-scale process improvement project.

In *Reengineering the Corporation: A Manifesto for Business Revolution*, Michael Hammer and James Champy identify business transformation as a top-down approach that focuses on strategic objectives.[1] Hammer and Champy's definition of business transformation is analogous to the Capability Assessment Model described in Chapter 4, where we showed how to identify processes that offer the most impact from an intervention. Business process reengineering (BPR) is more strategically focused, analogous to the intervention itself—the change that is actually made to improve the process. In a sense, business process reengineering can be thought of as a proxy for all process improvement methods, such as Lean, Six Sigma, and Total Quality Management. All of these methods are subsets of BPR, according to Hammer and Champy's definition.

The value-driven BPM approach to business transformation includes both the top-down strategic, boardroom level of thinking and the bottom-up view of the as-is state, an accurate description of the way things work today. Value-driven BPM can help identify fundamental areas that have problems, thus substantially affecting the business and helping practitioners decide where to conduct BPR. As we showed in Chapter 4, the analysis that produces a roadmap to value-driven BPM highlights objectively that some processes provide more value than others. Value-driven BPM provides focus and sustainability to process improvement efforts.

Conducting a roadmap analysis establishes which processes differentiate the organization in the marketplace, which are standard, and which are underdeveloped or simply missing. Process improvement methods can then be applied where the impact will be most critical. As we have stated, typically about 15 to 20 percent of processes are critical to companies' ability to differentiate themselves and excel in their markets; efforts should be focused on making these processes very effective.

Business Transformation Out of Context

As part of a business process transformation project, a transportation company designed a new order-management function and focused this function on combining production and financial information at the point of order entry. The object was to speed orders into production from the time the orders were created rather than wait to translate orders into production instructions later.

Unfortunately, the company only transformed the order-management function. It did not examine the entire end-to-end process of order-to-production. The company did not implement skills training in production issues or coordinate information from the production side. The project sat on a shelf, never to be implemented. Value-driven BPM would have helped to set that transformation in its proper context. It would also have helped the company to understand the complete picture, including all of the related processes, and to understand the impact on and required changes to people's skills and capabilities.

Another company optimized its sales process by removing all of the technical information in sales documents, only to be obligated to add extra manpower and time into the production department, collecting information that used to be gathered during the sales process. Because of the intense focus on optimizing one operation without consideration of the end-to-end process and its context, the sales-to-production cycle took a full week longer instead of gaining efficiency.

PROCESS IMPROVEMENT METHODS (BOTTOM-UP, PEOPLE-CENTRIC)

Value-driven BPM is complementary to process improvement methods because it provides a framework for choosing and deploying these techniques in a context that makes sense for the business as a whole. BPM reveals clues that may indicate that a certain process improvement method is most appropriate for a given situation.

Value-driven BPM can guide the intelligent application of a process improvement method such as Six Sigma or Lean to a people-centric process. Instead of pointing Six Sigma at every process, with value-driven BPM you can focus on processes that have the most impact, increasing the return on your investment.

Conversely, value-driven BPM also helps pinpoint processes that would benefit from scaling or new innovation. Six Sigma can be a powerful tool in a company that is run using value-driven BPM because it is used with greater precision. Even a general-purpose method such as *Kaizen* provides more benefit when used based on the principles of value-driven BPM.

Continuous Improvement Drives Profit for Chemical Manufacturer

Many companies have realized significant results establishing and running continuous improvement programs on their journeys toward operational excellence. In one such case, a global chemical manufacturer largely attributed an amazing two-year enterprise turnaround to its Operational Excellence program. Underpinning this program was robust problem solving through operations assessments, project portfolio development/prioritization, Lean Six Sigma capability building, deployment design, and execution. Paired with this execution capability was a focus on building an effective continuous improvement infrastructure, including champions, sponsors, and a Center of Excellence. There was also strong leadership support and advocacy, as well as the implementation of a rigorous performance management discipline that drove accountability for continuous improvement results. With an orchestrated effort on execution across the business—from sourcing, product development, and manufacturing to commercialization and all support functions—the company was able to drive more than 1 percent of its revenues to the bottom line, see quality improve and cycle times accelerate, and realize nearly a tenfold improvement in share price—attributed to consistent return of profits, improvement in working capital, and newfound investor confidence.

As described earlier in the chapter, there are many examples where continuous improvement programs have driven great value. How could the chemical manufacturer have done even better or positioned itself for even more growth with value-driven BPM? There would have been more than a few arguments to make in this case.

Formally documenting processes and establishing process ownership and governance along the way could have not only provided greater transparency, accelerated deployment, and supported compliance, but it could have also enabled a new quick-change capability (agility) in the organization. With the well-known adage that "the only constant is change" in mind, the development of such process assets and the establishment of a disciplined Process of Process Management could have made the continuing need to design, improve, and deploy processes even more efficient and robust. For example, the Process of Process Management enables efficiency because the need to map existing processes no longer exists. Rather than starting an improvement effort by mapping the current state, the previously agreed on or improved process could be displayed on the wall and gap assessment initiated immediately. Energy and effort could be focused on true process innovation rather than arguing about and investigating how it is truly done today. Moreover, with this new speed and agility of process change and improvement, changing market, customer, and regulatory requirements become opportunities rather than management distractions or business cost drivers.

With well-defined and documented processes, the next level of benefits from technology could have been realized. With process improvement and standardization comes the ability to leverage the benefits of automation, effectively locking in and even extending such benefits while providing a new ability to measure and monitor effectiveness.

Value-driven BPM effectively links business strategy and objectives with process and execution. Resources (people, time, money) are scarce, so their efforts need to be consistently focused and prioritized over time so that maximum return on investment is achieved. Such efforts are best aligned to specific strategic outcomes as well as refocused accordingly as business priorities change.

The lesson learned is that process improvement programs and business process management concepts go hand in hand: not only to help drive and sustain benefits and support an ongoing culture of process excellence, but also to offer new levels of business agility and process-based advantage. This is true even for the best continuous improvement programs, which may already be creating competitive advantage.

Value-driven BPM prioritizes efforts for continuous improvement as well as individual interventions. Once an organization returns from the upheaval of an intervention to the steady state of day-to-day operations, to keep the changes in place, and to continue to find new opportunities for improvement, discipline needs to be maintained.

Six Sigma on the Rampage

A public authority had spent six years implementing a Six Sigma program on a wide scale, with a requisite army of "black belts" sweeping through a large number of departments with ruthless efficiency—or so they thought. In our first appointment with leadership, our question was, "How has this affected the bottom line?" They told us they'd spent $15 million but could not explain how the bottom line had been improved. It wasn't a total loss—many processes had been significantly improved. But others had been streamlined when what was needed was knowledge and innovation. Downstream, that led to mistakes that required compensation in other departments. It became obvious that the "savings" promised by Six Sigma had been realized in part, but had actually raised complexity and cost in other areas. Six Sigma had led to incremental improvements in some existing processes but had fallen far short of the desired effects—in fact, new processes and significant changes to existing processes were required.

What happened? The organization had tried to improve all its processes simultaneously with Six Sigma. Once we were engaged, we were able to help leadership see the forest (outcomes of value tied to process improvements) through the trees (the obsessive work of process improvements in isolation). The organization then understood that value-driven BPM is about categorizing improvement efforts and highlighting alternate approaches to improving individual processes, including understanding where to direct their Six Sigma capability.

The positive news was that the organization had developed an excellent Six Sigma capability. Through process triangulation (as described in Chapter 4) and the use of complementary BPM tools—for example, simulation—the organization was able to realize real benefits quickly.

Value-driven BPM is a valid technique for prioritizing efforts at continuous improvement. The top-down analysis still applies, but the application of BPM tends to be at a lower, more granular level and intersects with process-improvement methods such as *Kaizen.*

The continuous repetition of the process value analysis, as described in Chapter 4, leads to continuous improvement, as the roadmap and process priorities are now permanently adjusted.

Continuous improvement is thus an integrated part of the Process of Process Management.

BPM and *Kaizen*

Kaizen focuses on small, achievable tasks that individuals at every level can accomplish to incrementally improve a process. Such efforts can benefit from prioritization. Rather than encouraging employees to "improve everything all the time," which can lead to an overtaxed workday, incomplete improvements, and the erosion of the morale that *Kaizen* is supposed to build, value-driven BPM can organize and structure improvement actions around critical value drivers. As *Kaizen* emphasizes teamwork, it is best if the goals around which it is centered are shared goals that are defensible and well understood. Value-driven BPM can identify those goals through determining the critical value drivers and working through the Process Improvement Matrix. If, for example, value-driven BPM identifies customer service improvement as a goal, the day-to-day improvement efforts of a *Kaizen* campaign can be focused around customer service. This increases the chances for measurable improvement.

VALUE-DRIVEN BPM AND IT TRANSFORMATIONS (TOP-DOWN, IT-CENTRIC)

Value-driven BPM also can insert value and process awareness into projects that are not normally thought to be strategic. For example, IT upgrades, such as the migration from one version of an ERP system to another, can have far greater impact when improvement projects are executed to improve processes core to value creation and to standardize those processes that support "context"—routine activities that every organization must carry out in order to continue operating.

Creating a roadmap, as outlined in Chapter 4, will likely uncover the fact that many processes are related to IT capabilities. And because of the pervasiveness of IT in most organizations, it's also likely that one or two IT improvements can affect many different processes. Practitioners are typically staring down a long list of IT improvements. Which will have the most impact? We can use value-driven BPM to make top-down IT-based efforts more effective.

Value-driven BPM can help prioritize IT capabilities based on their impact on value. The result is usually that the immature, high-impact capabilities get priority treatment. Value-driven BPM can help foster better understanding about how applications support business goals. Linking "what to do" as described in the process framework with "what technology to change, add, or improve" becomes a very useful exercise. For example, implementing routine IT upgrades provides an excellent opportunity to make upgrades more valuable, because it links the upgrades with outcomes the business desires.

One of the reasons the link between IT improvements and process is obscured has to do with changes in the software industry. The industry has changed from a consulting business that built custom applications to solve specific business problems to a commoditized industry that makes effective but highly standardized products. Many IT "transformations" today are essentially upgrades, which IT is expected to handle for the lowest cost with the least downtime.

This results in missed opportunities to improve processes and the IT environment along with them. When the goal is only to plug in a new technology for an existing process, there is no analysis of whether the process actually works before codifying it into an application that your company might have to live with for years.

Targeting the BPM Laser at a Major Global Services Company (Top-Down, IT-Centric Effort)

A major global services company was identifying applications to support processes at each of its businesses. During the capability assessment, the company discovered that several of its divisions used multiple applications to complete similar processes. The lack of standardization hurt the bottom line because of the IT support needed to upgrade and maintain many different applications.

Using an industry-specific reference model, the client worked with us to develop a customized methodology for documenting business processes, comparing the company's approach with its peers. The findings were stored in a BPM repository. Using the BPM community subprocess of BPM transformation, we trained a group of business-line and IT employees on the best ways to conduct workshops with subject-matter experts, extracting best practices for establishing a Center of Excellence. This helped the company make decisions about which applications to eliminate and helped it apply a process perspective to application development—drawing on the repository—so that future applications can be more closely aligned with business objectives.

In this case, the BPM laser was pointed only at a specific problem—redundant applications—which was actually costing the company money and whose remediation could save the company money going forward, while improving its process design and implementing a Process of Process Management—a discipline that can be applied in other areas of the company. Applying value-driven BPM helped make IT more effective across the company.

Value-Driven BPM: Mending the IT-Business Rift

Value-driven BPM can be an organizing technique for traditional technology landscapes, both in terms of creating a better overall understanding of how technology supports business processes and in terms of prioritizing changes to processes and the software that supports them.

With persistence, eventually one can create an IT infrastructure of tremendous agility, which eliminates a number of the obstacles between IT, execution, and business. An understanding of value-driven BPM can help IT determine priorities in a way that helps the business.

One of the key points made in Chapter 1 was that IT is growing in breadth but arriving in smaller chunks. One major challenge for CIOs is determining when a new IT capability is relevant to the business and when it can be ignored or evaluated later. Value-driven BPM provides the transparency to allow CIOs to confidently make such decisions. When evaluating a new technology, a CIO can start by looking at the short list of processes that are the focus of process improvement efforts. The CIO can then ask, "Will this capability improve any of the processes on the short list?" At first, this question will not be easy to answer. But after the CIO has done this analysis for a few technologies, the needs of the processes will become clearer. The CIO will know which capabilities would matter, what information would matter, which process steps take too long, and so forth. By understanding which processes are important and studying them, the CIO now has a powerful tool to sort through the explosion of new technology.

VALUE-DRIVEN BPM AND BOTTOM-UP, IT-CENTRIC IMPROVEMENTS

A process-centric view of IT prepares practitioners for a world that is adaptive to change. Instead of seeing IT only as technology infrastructure that is detached from process understanding and design, business analysts can package IT into a variety of services that support processes. This empowerment makes the cost of change lower because services can be combined and recombined as processes are adapted, and it expands the population of people who can build and adapt solutions. Often these solutions support a specific role that is participating in a process.

We can use the word *service* as a synonym for an application software component, delivering specific results needed to support one or several functions of a business process. These services help present IT as a process-focused asset because services abstract the underlying transaction systems. Services provide a much more flexible way of designing processes and incorporating those processes into IT than using a traditional command-and-control ERP system with custom extensions. Services can also call functions in an ERP system, allowing users or applications to simply call a function in ERP, provide some input or read some output, and store the results back if appropriate.

A simple example of a service is a real-time inventory check. Let's say you are playing a round of golf in September and hear a friend talking about the next big gift for the holiday season. You wonder how many you have in your stores and what you've got in the warehouse. You use your phone to quickly check on this. Behind the scenes, a service calls out to the ERP system and subtracts any stock sold via retail.

Effectively, organizations can create a service-oriented architecture (SOA) that provides direct access to services in a tangible format and abstracts the underlying transactional systems. Practitioners can then begin embedding knowledge, expertise, and policies for running the business in more configurable forms of IT, such as rules engines. (A more detailed discussion of the role of service-oriented architecture can be found in Chapter 7.)

The increasing abstraction of process design from the underlying technology is a benefit to practitioners of value-driven BPM because the focus can more easily shift from making technology-based decisions about process (such as designing or changing processes around the limitations of the software) to making decisions about process based on value outcomes. The design and execution of processes become more closely aligned, and the Process of Process Management improves in tandem with the changes.

Here again, there is a potential pitfall of surgically improving a single process in a way that cuts off circulation to the rest of the body.

Acceleration Without Direction

An insurance company embarked on an ambitious project to speed the processing of claims. The plan was to automate claims processing from beginning to end. The "quick and dirty" project was so focused on acceleration that the practitioners ignored the fact that the company processed seven different types of claims while the automated system they chose could only handle three of them. That meant assigning people at the front end of the process to determine which claims could be automated and which could not, and to manually handle the nonautomated claims at the back end of the process, creating additional work rather than saving effort. With a value-driven BPM perspective, the company would have been able to identify all of the objects in the process and been able to define optimal targets for automation and plan accordingly.

The point of the discussion in this chapter is quite simple. Companies do not have to make a choice between Six Sigma, Lean, or any other process improvement technique and value-driven BPM. It is possible and advisable to say yes to both and move to a high level of process-centricity.

Note

1. Michael Hammer and James Champy, *Reengineering the Corporation: A Manifesto for Business Revolution* (New York: HarperBusiness, 1994).

PART II

Building a Value-Driven Organization

CHAPTER 6

Building an Organization for Value-Driven BPM

This chapter discusses the organization you'll need to put in place to support value-driven BPM, while Chapter 7 describes technological tools for value-driven BPM, and Chapter 8 discusses the management of process models, reference models, and your process repository.

Nothing happens unless it is someone's responsibility to make it happen. Nothing happens repeatedly unless it is embedded in the organization. If value-driven BPM is going to be more than a one-time project, the parts of the organization in the capability model mentioned in Chapter 1 will have to absorb BPM so that it becomes part of the way things get done. In addition, there should exist somewhere in the company a central cognitive function that is directing and guiding all of the distributed parts of BPM that have been absorbed, just as, for example, HR is represented through a centralized organization that oversees the various HR processes carried out in the organization.

In other words, in order to treat BPM as a management discipline, with all of the attendant responsibilities, tasks, and playbooks, a management organization for BPM should be established. In most cases, the BPM Center of Excellence (CoE) is this organization. The CoE is charged with providing governance over the Process of Process Management and exploring how it can be integrated into an organization. The CoE is the brain, so to speak, that masterminds and coordinates the implementation of value-driven BPM.

The word *integrated* is key. BPM and many related process improvement initiatives have not taken hold in the way they were intended because too much of the advanced thinking about process stays inside a locked box and is not built into the broader organization's daily life. Therefore, the role of the CoE is not only to create process excellence but also to champion and enforce it throughout the organization. The CoE leads the process through which other parts of the company absorb BPM. Remember, it doesn't happen all at once. Part of that education campaign involves empowering roles outside the CoE to contribute learning and integration of process excellence in the day-to-day lives of everyone in the organization. When this happens, "the BPM organization" is no longer a separate group—it is part of each unit of the organization. Process is a competitive advantage, and its elevated importance becomes part of the corporate identity.

The road to this future state has challenges, but they are surmountable. Practitioners of value-driven BPM will struggle with such questions as

- How can our organization ensure that our BPM capability is more than a group sitting in the background producing process models and reports?
- How can our organization ensure that our BPM efforts are at the forefront of the business change agenda and linked to value?

The CoE needs to think of the organization as a market to be served. This kind of thinking reminds everyone that process excellence brings value when it is connected to tangible outcomes—outcomes for which there is a market. Value-driven BPM cannot be forced on a company. True absorption comes from creating true believers by creating business success.

Part of the cultural imperative behind value-driven BPM is leadership from management. The clue is in the definition—"management discipline." Value-driven BPM is driven by management and supported by the CoE. The head of the CoE is, of course, part of management.

As the lead champion of process excellence, the CoE fosters cultural change in the organization to support value-driven BPM. This is a step that many companies miss, resulting in roles and assets that are unutilized, in effect a brain with no arms or limbs. A well-executed culture and change management program will maximize the usefulness of the pragmatic capabilities being developed.

> How important is it to have a process organization? Of organizations that implemented BPM successfully, 94 percent had a formal Center of Excellence or process management organization. Of those, 67 percent said BPM exceeded their expectations.[1]

WHAT IS A PROCESS ORGANIZATION AND WHY DO I NEED IT?

To give value-driven BPM a place in your company, you need to foster a process-centric culture, suffused with people who help move value-driven BPM forward. There are three main components of a process organization: the CoE, the process organization, and a process-centric culture.

The BPM Center of Excellence

The BPM Center of Excellence can be centralized, decentralized, or a combination. The CoE is the core unit responsible for the successful implementation and ongoing maintenance of the Process of Process Management, executing its core activities. The point of origin and departmental location of the CoE will vary from company to company, but there is no question that you will need an organization, however small to begin with, to own the Process of Process Management.

"But We Don't Need a BPM Organization"

We recently spoke with a couple of board members at a client company, and they said, "Well, you talk about this BPM organization and Center of Excellence and all that, but do we really need it? Why don't we just institute your Process of Process Management in our organization and that's it? We have BPM in every department. We don't need a BPM organization."

We explained, "You could say the same thing about your HR department. You have people in every department, they have to get paid, you have to do performance reviews, and you have to do training. Your HR department supports all of this. It executes some work itself and delivers standards and guidelines for others.

"It's the same with BPM. If you want to roll out processes efficiently in your organization, see synergies, and apply them in the right way, you need people who take care of that, and those people are in the process organization."

The CoE devotes the majority of its time to implementing value-driven BPM and directing the PoPM. The CoE defines a variety of roles related to the definition, propagation, and continuous improvement of the PoPM. The CoE is supported by the rest of the organization through its general behaviors as well as through specific leadership roles, depending on the scale and the distribution of authority. The CoE may be centralized and support your entire company. It might have a more distributed structure, with satellite groups, individual organizational units, or geographic divisions. To adopt value-driven BPM, your Center of Excellence does not necessarily need to be a completely separate unit. For example, it could be a function of your operations or IT department—the two departments most frequently affected by process improvement.

The day-to-day activities of the CoE are based on the organization's needs and the stage of adoption of value-driven BPM. If a little more transparency is all that is needed, the main role of the Center of Excellence might be to create and maintain a repository to give everyone across the organization more visibility into processes. The CoE should always include the basic components of BPM operations (see Chapter 3). Any process changes are submitted to the CoE, which keeps them up-to-date.

A CoE might start with just a few people and then grow. Roles in the beginning might include the following:

- CoE lead
- Process architect
- Process modeler
- Tool administrator

However, in many organizations, especially at the outset of a value-driven BPM effort, one person may in fact play several of these roles. If you think about how an HR department evolves, you see a similar pattern. When a company starts, the CEO might sign all the paychecks or just have the accountant or comptroller do it. But as the company grows, an HR department is needed. Similarly, your organization will grow as you develop a more extensive BPM capability throughout your company and as value-driven BPM efforts increase. Over time, you are creating a real asset of value that needs effective management.

> Without a CoE, centralized repositories and other BPM tools (though valuable in their own right) are likely to become a stale collection of best-practice documents. Too many companies purchase software or extensively document processes with no clear goals or communication around the effort and wonder why no one bothers to look at the 600 process models they have created. Creating data or content without implementing a process to use it is wasteful. For example, who would create a parts database while ignoring the purchasing process?

The Process Organization

If the CoE is at the center, the next layer in the value-driven BPM model is the process organization, which refers to the parts of the company that absorb BPM into their way of doing business. Incorporating the CoE, but expanding further into the company, the process organization consists of process owners in various departments, such as IT, procurement, and human resources, all of which should be closely aligned with the CoE. Each unit in the process organization has some direct tie through which it formally supports a part of the PoPM.

For example, the CoE interacts with business, so it needs advocates for the PoPM such as process owners. It interacts with IT, so it needs IT roles to support it. The exact nature of your process organization will depend on your needs.

A Process Culture

The third, widest, and most comprehensive group is less of a formal organization than a way of thinking that is informed and reinforced by the activities of the CoE and the process organization. A process culture spans the entire organization. It helps people understand how their individual work fits into the larger context of value-driven BPM. When people choose to use the tools of BPM because they know that they help save time and ensure that what they do will have a lasting impact that is aligned with a company's strategy, a process culture is clearly in place. People in a process culture understand how the concept of an end-to-end business process provides value to clients and how their individual roles impact that value. Ideally, any organization practicing value-driven BPM incorporates those principles in the job roles of every individual. A process culture is key to the success of value-driven BPM, yet it is probably the most difficult to measure. Later in this chapter, we suggest some approaches for establishing this culture in the organization.

BUILDING A CENTER OF EXCELLENCE TO PROVIDE PROCESS GOVERNANCE

The right way to build a Center of Excellence depends heavily on the personality of a company. In some firms, all victories are victories of centralization. In other firms, major victories come from distributing power to be exercised according to guidelines. Creating a CoE to implement value-driven BPM needs to be done in a way that is compatible with the company's existing way of thinking. The shape of the CoE is somewhat different at each organization we have encountered.

Ultimately, one common element of all CoEs regardless of the form they take is that they are the owners of the Process of Process Management. The CoE is like a dynamic switching center where you throw the value switch, which helps spotlight best practices as your organization follows the roadmap to value-driven BPM, as outlined in Chapter 4. The BPM operations subprocess of the PoPM is the first iteration of the CoE in most companies. As the steward of BPM operations, the CoE creates and maintains the roadmap.

As you establish a CoE, here are a few things to keep in mind. First, you will likely uncover new roles and responsibilities as you build your BPM capability—thinking about restructuring processes often leads to a redesign of the relationships between people and the work they do. The new roles may be in the CoE to carry out the PoPM or in the rest of the company to either carry out the PoPM or to better perform operational processes.

Origins and Growth Patterns of the BPM CoE

The CoE can grow organically and can start on a small scale, as described earlier, such as building up capabilities around one process. When new requests come down the line that clearly have organization-wide implications, such as automation, rather than having each business unit take responsibility for the project, the company might decide to centralize its efforts through the CoE. With every new component of the PoPM, the CoE has new offerings, or products and services, it can bring to the organization—its "market." With those new offerings come new roles and responsibilities, and with the addition of these roles, the organizational structure changes.

The CoE develops differently in every organization. It can start with a group in IT that is heavily focused on integration topics. This group then may pull in missing competencies from lines of business. The CoE could also start with a group of traditional process improvement practitioners in the chief operating officer's organization. As these practitioners take a broader view, they may reach out to other divisions to grow the CoE. In still other organizations, the CEO may decide that the organization needs to develop a Center of Excellence centrally, on a clean slate, and hand the task to the senior vice president of strategy. That person may in turn reach out to operations and IT to support critical elements of the strategy.

In general, it's useful to start with an existing group that has some common interest in BPM so that a process culture does not have to be built from scratch. Regardless of how or where it begins, the CoE typically grows and expands its reach into many other departments, as value-driven BPM is an organization-wide management discipline. But the CoE could start virtually anywhere.

Despite the necessity of a CoE to own the PoPM, provide guidance, and give process development a shape and direction, process capabilities are not simply visited on an organization from above. The creation of the CoE can be top down, bottom up, or a combination, depending on the nature of the company.

Even though the CoE grows organically, growth is not automatic. It takes effort to create and sustain an effective CoE. Practices, people, and tools have to be connected in a meaningful way in order for the PoPM to continue to have its desired impact in facilitating value-driven BPM.

Typical Organizational Approaches to Centers of Excellence

There are three key approaches to embedding BPM CoEs in the organization: centralized, decentralized, and hybrid (Figure 6-1).

In the centralized approach, there is one CoE for the entire organization. Everything is handled centrally and synergies are maximized. Delivery is standardized and consistent. There is greater process visibility and a single point of contact responsible. Japanese organizations, for example, where the business culture is built around centralization, have had success with this approach.

The centralized approach provides tight control of the PoPM. The disadvantages include less flexibility for local geographies and business lines to customize the deliverables of the PoPM for particular situations. Sometimes, activities of the CoE can be seen as imperious, or being done "to" down-the-line participants and processes, rather than as collaborative efforts. Skills may be seen as too centralized and out of touch with the edges of the organization. The utilization of the team may be uneven, leaving some groups idle for long periods while others are extremely busy.

The decentralized approach places a CoE in each business unit or in each geographical division. The main advantage here is the proximity and close connection with particular regions or to particular business lines. The CoE can be better customized to each unit's particular needs and can be directly embedded in projects that are highly relevant to each unit. The business line tends to feel a high degree of ownership over the CoE in this case.

However, much of the synergistic effect of shared best practices is lost with the decentralized approach. Accountability is diffuse, skills are scattered, dependencies are obscured, and the organization may be inconsistent between business units.

The highly decentralized model does not work in most companies because it makes it difficult to transfer knowledge between business units and internationally. The best use case for this model is in companies that are already highly decentralized, such as a group of companies under a holding-company umbrella, whose purpose may be to quickly buy and sell other entities for a profit.

Many organizations choose a hybrid approach to BPM CoEs. As the name implies, the hybrid approach combines the centralized and decentralized approaches. In this case, the CoE has a relatively small, centralized unit that focuses on BPM governance: enterprise-wide modeling standards, governance definitions, infrastructure, and repositories, for example. It probably also has a shared pool of process design and implementation specialists. BPM delivery is covered by the individual, regional, or product units so that client connectivity and locally optimized standards and infrastructure can be maintained.

The advantages of the hybrid approach: Knowledge is easily reused, access to process expertise is good, resources are well utilized, and a sense of participation is fostered between business units and the CoE (in other words, they feel they are building process capabilities "with" the CoE, rather than "for" the CoE).

The disadvantages of the hybrid approach: There is some risk of inconsistent application of process change, contacts between owners and implementers may be diffuse or obscure, and accountabilities are also more diffuse than in highly centralized approaches.

Once the structure of the CoE is defined, the next task is to determine how the structure fits best into the organization. Whatever path is chosen, the relationships between other organizational units and the CoE should be explicitly detailed.

The CoE role is analogous to that of IT, which is a capability used throughout a company. In some companies, IT and the CIO report directly to the CEO. In others, depending on the prominence of technology in an organization and the availability of the CEO, the CIO reports to a financial function, such as the CFO. In still others, the role of technology is so important to each individual department that a generic IT department reports to either the CEO or the CFO, and each line of business has a captive Center of Excellence

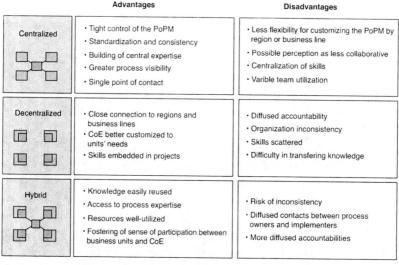

	Advantages	Disadvantages
Centralized	· Tight control of the PoPM · Standardization and consistency · Building of central expertise · Greater process visibility · Single point of contact	· Less flexibility for customizing the PoPM by region or business line · Possible perception as less collaborative · Centralization of skills · Varible team utilization
Decentralized	· Close connection to regions and business lines · CoE better customized to units' needs · Skills embedded in projects	· Diffused accountability · Organization inconsistency · Skills scattered · Difficulty in transfering knowledge
Hybrid	· Knowledge easily reused · Access to process expertise · Resources well-utilized · Fostering of sense of participation between business units and CoE	· Risk of inconsistency · Diffused contacts between process owners and implementers · More diffused accountabilities

FIGURE 6-1. Approaches to Building a Center of Excellence

dedicated to meeting its own needs with technology. The same is true with process.

We are very often asked, "Where should we place our new Center of Excellence?" Our simple response to this question is often, "Place the CoE where it will get the most oxygen and truly provide a cross-organizational service." This is a different place in every organization.

In general, the right placement for a CoE is specific to the conditions at any organization. In an ideal situation, where BPM is truly seen as a management discipline, it is a top-level position and may even be led by a C-level executive, such as a chief process officer (CPO)—a role discussed in more detail in Chapter 10. We see three main cases in practice:

- The BPM CoE reports directly to the board.
- The CoE is part of the CIO's organization.
- The CoE is part of the COO's organization.

Wherever the CoE is located, it can be implemented using a centralized, decentralized, or hybrid approach.

GOVERNANCE ORGANIZATIONS OUTSIDE THE CENTER OF EXCELLENCE

Although the CoE is intended to guide and manage the implementation of process in the organization, it is critical for the rest of the organization to adopt a process approach as well. This can be achieved by establishing a BPM governance capability that provides guidance for the champions and leaders of value-driven BPM adoption in each part of the organization. Governance processes help define the relationship between the CoE and the rest of the company and also make sure that people feel empowered to act on their own.

The process for developing a BPM governance capability can be executed using RACI, a process for defining who is *responsible*, who is *accountable*, who should be *consulted*, and who should be *informed*.[2] These processes can help set a course for governing BPM in your organization.

When building the CoE, it is helpful to be cognizant of two basic setups. There is a "pure management" approach, which is more reactive and deferential to the rest of the organization, and a "proactive" approach, in which the CoE asserts itself and sets the agenda for management practices throughout the organization. Many organizations add governing bodies like process committees, representing, for example, the owners of all major processes. It is best to select the CoE approach that meshes with the overall character and process needs of your organization; a culture clash that begins right at the outset of creating a CoE is not likely to yield positive results.

The BPM CoE's interactions with other parts of the organization should be explicitly stated. Let's take a moment to walk through the RACI aspects of the BPM governance subprocess.

Questions to ask include, "How do the units interact?" and "What happens if a process has to be changed?" For example, suppose the process owner in the business unit is *responsible* for initiating the change. The CoE is *accountable* for executing on that change, including the analysis of the existing process and design of the change. The CoE *consults* with experts on the business and *informs* management or other people impacted by the initiative. To implement the solution, there are multiple paths, depending on the organization. If the solution is purely organizational, the implementation could be driven by the business units and supported by the CoE. If the implementation heavily involves IT, then IT can drive the process, with CoE support, ensuring that the change follows process guidelines. In both of these cases, the CoE is consulted and informed about the changes but is not the leader of those changes.

The CoE acts mainly as a pure management unit, which waits to accept triggers from process owners and maintains a repository of processes that reflects learning from the requests it fulfills. Generally the pure management CoE needs only to be consulted and informed, in RACI parlance.

In some organizations, the CoE may actually dominate the RACI chart, taking a great deal of responsibility and accountability for process development. Typically, value-driven BPM leads to a proactive CoE, which does not solely wait for requests from process owners but may initiate changes as well. It is also a continuous research facility that procures reference models from other industries and provides actionable insights on business change. For example, a telecommunications provider with a large wireless business might be interested in using reference models from the retail world to better organize store displays. The CoE can drive such an initiative, helping the organization to learn from other industries.

EXAMPLE ROLES AND RESPONSIBILITIES

The makeup of a BPM organization varies widely. Table 6-1 lists typical roles with associated organizational scope, functions, and objectives, as well as the area of the PoPM to which they provide assistance. Note that many BPM organizations transition from an operational, tactical group in an existing department to a separate department over time. During the growth period, several roles may be attached to a single person before the BPM organization expands into more permanent positions. Roles here do not mean job titles or job descriptions. Eventually, the BPM organization may grow to the point that it needs dedicated full-time employees for some roles. Also note that not everyone in the BPM organization would "work" in the CoE; process roles and responsibilities should exist across the company and work with those in the CoE.

This list is not exhaustive—some organizations have many more roles attached to BPM (and many have just a few key roles). But these roles are typical in our experience.

TABLE 6-1. Roles in the BPM Organization

Role	Function	Objectives (Area of PoPM)
Business process owner	Management	Oversees process from end to end, identifies where improvements need to be made, and approves any changes or new projects; top role in the governance area of the PoPM
Business sponsor	Management	Champions business case and secures funding for projects
CoE leader	Management	Oversees BPM CoE, including operations and other relevant subprocesses; the "head of the PoPM"
Process architect	Operational	Maintains knowledge, standards, and tools (BPM methods and tools, BPM delivery)

TABLE 6-1. Roles in the BPM Organization. *continued*

Role	Function	Objectives (Area of PoPM)
Process designer	Operational	Performs process modeling (BPM delivery)
Application architect	Operational	Designs technical infrastructure (BPM methods and tools, BPM delivery)
Data architect	Operational	Designs data integration (BPM methods and tools, BPM delivery)
Change management lead	Management/ Operational	Defines the change management strategy and approach and manages its execution across the organization (BPM transformation, BPM delivery)
Delivery manager	Management	Selects project-management methods and approach (BPM transformation); applies project management methods to specific projects (BPM delivery)
Partner manager	Management	Coordinates external partners, for example, software or consulting firms (BPM methods and tools)
Project team members	Operational	Drive process change in BPM delivery
Project portfolio manager	Operational	Manages the portfolio of process improvement projects; drives the continuous improvement program
Project-related business stakeholders	Management	Responsible for meeting KPIs and ensuring success of a BPM project (BPM delivery)
V-BPM business stakeholders	Management	Responsible for building the BPM organization and the PoPM (BPM transformation); BPM operations; BPM governance
Technical support	Operational	Troubleshoots issues with specific tools (BPM methods and tools)
Repository administrator	Operational	Manages the repository from a tech/tool perspective (BPM methods and tools)
Business process improvement expert	Operational	Specializes in a process improvement technique such as *Kaizen* or Six Sigma (BPM methods and tools; BPM delivery)

BPM CULTURE AND CHANGE MANAGEMENT _____

Creating an organization for value-driven BPM is a major step forward toward institutionalizing the PoPM. But if you plan to reach the highest level of value-driven BPM maturity, you need to consider how to make BPM part of your overall organizational culture.

Of course, even if your organizational culture is not ready for BPM, training in process management can be very effective in preparing an organization for change. Basic change management skills are paramount, as is a structure that takes into account the business, tools, and context in which you want to build your process organization. (Note, however, that this chapter provides an overview of culture and change management in the context of value-driven BPM; a complete treatment of this subject is beyond the scope of this book.)

BPM Culture

Culture is a word that can mean many things. To our understanding, a culture of BPM would be in place if, at the beginning of discussions about what went wrong with a process, or how to improve a process, the participants instinctively asked themselves:

- What is the process that we are all involved in?
- Has that process been agreed on?
- Has that process been changed?
- Have we understood that process in the same way?
- Have we confirmed our understanding?
- Has the process been designed with a focus on customer experience?
- Has that process been tuned to make sure that it is representing the largest goals of the organization, the strategy of the organization, and the value that needs to be created to justify the execution of that strategy?

If all participants are thinking this way, we have made a great start toward a BPM culture, but we have not completed our journey. To make such an awareness work, we also need other aspects of that culture to be in place. BPM culture is a way of thinking about the cultural characteristics you need to make BPM happen effectively. Some defining characteristics include the following:

- A culture of customer and market focus
- A culture of collaboration and integration
- A culture of open communication
- A culture of mutual respect
- A culture of innovation
- A culture that understands the relationship of process to daily activities

A process culture can answer the following questions:

- What does it feel like to be process-centric?
- What does it feel like when value-driven BPM is working for you?

When such a culture is embedded in the organization, everyone understands the final outcome of a process and how it affects external and internal clients. As a result, everyone can understand how to impact the result of value and focus on common goals.

Collaboration and Integration

A process culture helps people understand how the individual work they carry out fits into the larger context of value-driven BPM and how an end-to-end business process provides value to clients. To achieve this, everyone in a process-centric culture has a distinct understanding of how their daily tasks actually provide value to clients. (This can include internal clients as well, such as any employee who is a "customer" of IT or HR.) Through such integration, these employees see the value of their work in a way that may not have been clear before.

Transparency leads to awareness of the big picture, how all the parts of a company and of specific processes fit together. Employees also see how their roles interact with those of their coworkers (or increasingly, counterparts in another company who are part of the same value chain) in a process to deliver results of value. If there is clarity about how each step of a process connects to the next, workers will be more motivated to understand the nuances of handoffs from one person or department to the next, for example. Partners need to be able to exchange ideas, trade suggestions, and have a complete view of a process from end to end.

To achieve this clarity, explicit communication and a specific understanding of process ownership and responsibilities are required. It should be clear who has end-to-end responsibility for improving process for the organization as a whole, solving process issues for the entire organization rather than solving for just one part.

Innovation

New ideas happen when people not only work to solve their own problems but also contribute to help others solve problems, as well as when people think about how the overall process impacts the client. Product and process innovation are the outcomes of an environment that encourages collaboration and communication.

A BPM culture can be thought of like a jazz combo performing a song. There is always room for improvisation, so long as the solos are in the right key, support the overall structure of the tune, and don't throw the entire composition off course. Each participant is vital to the overall performance and compensates for others by reducing or increasing his or her role at key moments. For each part led by a certain instrument, there is an opportunity for that individual or group to create and innovate, but fundamentally, everyone is looking at the same sheet of music. The dynamic between leading and following, between innovating and subjugating to a structure, is exactly what's needed in a BPM culture. And, like a jazz combo, each organization may play the same standard (retail clothing, banking, manufacturing, etc.) in a slightly different way, but in such a way that differentiates that organization and provides unique value.

Process Training

Information, communication, and training are needed to prepare the organization to support the PoPM as it matures. Initially, there may be training on a limited scope, such as allowing a trainee to see the process models in a repository. Later, there may be more sophisticated training, such as how to analyze a process based on its performance against process models.

Two types of training support value-driven BPM; each reflects a different leg of the triangulation concept (see Triangulation on the next page). On one leg, the process organization and the CoE should be trained to implement the Process of Process Management (as described in Chapters 3 and 4) and to take care of value-driven

BPM as a management discipline. On the other leg, process training relates to the practitioners who will be implementing value-driven BPM within the processes themselves, such as sales or procurement.

Triangulation

You can improve your BPM skills at the same time you improve a specific process. When building a process organization, you will get the most benefit when you derive best practices of process management from the point problems that you solve. We call this "triangulation." This is one of the roles of the process organization—to make sure practitioners don't just "fix it and forget it." Instead, we encourage you to fix it, document it, and share what you learned. A more detailed description of this concept can be found in Chapter 4.

In either case, the structure of the training is approximately the same. But as with any training, it helps when people understand how it fits into the larger business. Triangulation can be a helpful concept for explaining to practitioners whether they are being trained in learning value-driven BPM as a management discipline or are executing an aspect of the PoPM in the context of an operational process.

In either case, there can be no better example of the value of the process organization than to use the principles of BPM in the training process. We recommend using process models as part of a common "language of change." The language of change mediates between the different perspectives of the stakeholders in change management, such as business analysts, managers, executives, IT personnel, and consultants. Using a formal method, such as event-driven process chains (EPCs), helps to provide clear communication.[3]

Training needs a specific structure. There are four types of training needed by the business units:[4]

* *Basic business training:* This type of training explains the reason for change and the new business skills needed. For example, a manufacturing firm that switches from manual materials requirement planning (MRP) to an ERP solution may need employees to make more complex decisions about parts ordering, based on minimum stock or other parameters.

This work requires more developed business skills, and training should address those skills.

- *Enabler training:* This type of training provides an introduction to new technologies or other tools for the new or changed processes. This includes new software products or process performance tools. Such training generally takes more of a "how to use the software" approach than a "what to do with it" approach.

- *Business process training:* This category of training empowers people to do their new or modified jobs in the changed process environment. Training explains how to execute, monitor, and control processes. Depending on the project, it may also be appropriate to include process improvement training. The goal is to provide an integrated understanding of the end-to-end business process so that everyone understands the impact of his or her work on others and on the final result for the customer. Value-driven BPM is achieved when all people understand and deliver their impact on the desired outcomes.

- *Go-live training:* This training type explains how to prepare people for the execution of a new process, acknowledging the likelihood that the "soft launch" of the process may not go 100 percent smoothly. Go-live training may involve communicating a set of workarounds for anticipated issues and a call-escalation list of responsible parties for troubleshooting.

Incorporate Enabling Technology in the Training

To get the maximum benefit of business process training, incorporate specific enabling technology as part of the training. Trainees can get necessary background information, submit questions, and learn about the process. In other words, letting people experiment with process models and see how altering the models affects workflows and relationships can help them understand how process changes work in action. This training technique can be accomplished through ever-more-sophisticated computer-based training and distributed through social media. The latter is a fast-growing area described more at the end of Chapter 7 and again in Chapter 10.

Letting users test-drive enabling technology to see how workflows are affected in advance dovetails with the idea of lifetime

CHAPTER 6 · Building an Organization for Value-Driven BPM   119

learning and continuous training. Building training into the rhythm
of work prepares the organization for the future and makes change
less uncomfortable. It also makes value-driven BPM part of the daily
execution of processes.

Smooth Change Management for a Process Culture

Change management is defined as the combination of information,
communication, and training.[5] Volumes have been written about
change management, including books by Michael Hammer and others. We do not purport to address this issue in any great detail here;
rather, we briefly place it in the context of value-driven BPM.

We have found that the Architecture of Integrated Information
Systems (ARIS), developed by August-Wilhelm Scheer, can be useful in communicating changes in processes during training.[6] We use
this model because it reflects process-centricity particularly well. See
Chapter 7 for a detailed discussion of this model.

It's too easy to purchase a lot of software, or exhaustively document processes, while failing to achieve the BPM capability desired
by the organization. The abstractions that are a product of process
thinking should never lead us to lose sight of the core of the organizations that we want to change—people. Understanding the dynamics
and role changes that come with building up a BPM organization is
the key to success and a harmonious working environment. There is
no one-size-fits-all approach to building up your BPM organization.
Some organizations are more centralized than others. Some con-
centrate knowledge at the top and trickle it down; in others, it rises
upward like steam. But the skillful application of the generalities
discussed in this chapter, combined with specific knowledge of the
context of your process change and a deep and thorough understanding of your organization's culture—its *people*—will help you prevail.

Notes

1. Ken Vollner, "The EA View: BPM Has Become Mainstream," Forrester,
   October 2008.

2. Royston Morgan, "How to Do RACI Charting and Analysis: A Practical
   Guide," Project Smart, UK, accessed September 26, 2011, http://www
   .projectsmart.co.uk.

3. Mathias Kirchmer and August-Wilhelm Scheer, "Change Management: Key for Business Process Excellence," in *Business Process Change Management: ARIS in Practice,* ed. August-Wilhelm Scheer et al. (Berlin: Springer-Verlag, 2003), 23–48.

4. Mathias Kirchmer, *High-Performance Through Process Excellence,* 2nd ed. (Berlin: Springer-Verlag, 2011).

5. Ibid.

6. Mathias Kirchmer and August-Wilhelm Scheer, "Change Management: Key for Business Process Excellence," 1–14.

Information Technology for Value-Driven BPM

While one of the most common mistakes made when attempting to adopt BPM is falling in love with the available tools and making them the focus of the effort, a "no-tools" approach will, in the long term, also fail just as surely. This chapter continues our focus on the technological components of value-driven BPM with a discussion of the benefits you can derive from the many tools available. Our discussion is not centered on the detailed workings of the various tools that form the technical infrastructure for BPM; instead, we are focused on how the tools are positioned as a component of the overall value-driven BPM approach, linking them to strategic and operational value.

This chapter looks at the role of process models, modeling and repository tools, process management execution systems, and service-oriented architecture, revealing how these tools and technologies fit into the overall value story of BPM. We also discuss process performance monitoring. Typically, BPM gets a lot of emphasis when a new system is designed and implemented, and the related processes are mapped in parallel. But value-driven BPM takes into account how these monitoring capabilities play a critical role in continuing to drive value throughout the process life cycle. Organizations that do not measure their results—or measure only the conventional numbers—risk missing the information or value they need. This chapter explains how organizations can position this capability to measure and understand quickly what their various processes are doing, enabling them to use that information to drive the value agenda. We discuss the value of monitoring and management techniques, and process-mining techniques, in the context of knowing "what and how to measure" in order to control the processes, including the Process of Process Management, in the appropriate way.

The chapter concludes with a discussion about how organizations can use social BPM, supported by the latest wave in BPM technology, to drive value as well.

WHAT KIND OF TECHNOLOGY SUPPORTS VALUE-DRIVEN BPM?

Every business process needs tools. For example, taking and filling orders requires an order entry system. But without the orders, the system is useless. Just like a library without books, or a bank without money, repositories that support value-driven BPM are not useful without data in the form of process and related information models. Further, it is essential to pinpoint and spend time on the most relevant and appropriate process models. It is neither necessary nor advisable to model everything under the sun.

> We recently visited a company that understood the importance of process and was proud of its two-year program to model the business. The only difficulty was that no one could tell us how the models were going to be used or what level of detail was optimal. Nevertheless, the leaders assured us, "In two years, this will be great!"

The Process of Process Management can start manually, but to become most useful, it will soon require IT support, as any other management discipline or operational process does. Some of the components of the PoPM reference model do not require a great deal of IT support or sophisticated software. The BPM operations area, for example, may be initially best handled using simple worksheet-based tools.

Applying BPM to operational processes usually does require software tools. The PoPM leverages BPM software to *create, change, or improve* operational processes, such as those related to research and development, procurement, and human resources.

Other common platforms at many companies, such as the ERP system, *manage* the operational processes and can be part of a value-driven BPM initiative. BPM practitioners can recommend changes to the ERP system to improve a procurement process.

Whether an organization is using software explicitly created to implement BPM or some other tool that engages with a process, the most important success factor is having an accurate, structured description of processes that guides the process-oriented use of the tools and software in support of value-driven BPM. Many BPM technology implementations fail, not because the technology is poor but because the process models are either nonexistent or incorrect. When this happens, important aspects of the process are omitted from the implementation, such as information about people. Or, in the rush to correctly implement a piece of software, the organization may be closing itself off to ideas that may never have been incorporated into the technological infrastructure of the company—but that should have been.

In the 1990s, a utility was looking for a new process for cost distribution. We did some research and located a doctoral thesis from the early 1930s. The thesis had received poor marks because the algorithm it proposed for cost distribution was too unwieldy to be practical. But with the advances in computing power, the algorithm was much easier to implement and incorporate in business processes, and it became an important part of the cost-distribution process at the company.

A contrasting case would be the use of technology with no associated value outcome. An automotive parts manufacturer implemented an ERP system. Practitioners were eager to use the application's highly detailed bill of materials and routing capability, even though the company produced products with a very simple structure. Suddenly, the amount of administrative work increased dramatically because for every step in the routing process, people had to record the step's duration and enter product feedback, which they did not have to do before. Entering a very simple bill of materials would have sufficed and enabled automation without unnecessary steps. Here was a case of letting complex functionality of the software dictate process design, making it less efficient.

From this point forward, we examine the major categories of information technology tools used to support value-driven BPM.

PROCESS MODELING AND REPOSITORY TOOLS

The core of any BPM infrastructure is the process modeling and repository tool, which is one of the major drivers of transparency and ultimately broader awareness of the shape of business processes. It is the master data management tool for all BPM-related content, and it feeds all other BPM systems. Just like any other software platform, BPM repositories are only as good as the data that is entered into them. BPM applications deliver on their promise only when the right content governance and modeling guidelines are in place to help guide the content through the system. If a process changes, it has to be able to percolate through the system without causing a crisis. To be incorporated smoothly, the process, and the management of changes to the process, needs to be part of an overall Process of Process Management.

Table 7-1 lists the common process modeling and repository tools that we see in the market. (Gartner has also included most of these tools in a recent "magic quadrant."[1]) This is not intended to be a complete list but merely illustrates the types of tools and the typical scope of functions supported.

TABLE 7-1. Examples of Process Modeling and Repository Tools

Product/Company	Description
ARIS Software AG	In many ways still the market leader, with a rich metamodel. A modeling tool that integrates with SAP Solution Manager and Enterprise Service Repository, as well as Oracle Fusion and the webMethods process automation engine; most comprehensive functionality and available reference models.
Corporate Modeler Suite Casewise	Tool includes rich metamodels and industry-specific frameworks. Strength in UK public sector.
IBM Rational System Architect IBM	Includes portfolio management, BPM, and asset management as well as repository tools.

TABLE 7-1. Examples of Process Modeling and Repository Tools, *continued*

Product/Company	Description
MEGA Suite MEGA	Modeling suite includes multifeatured metamodel out of the box, as well as governance, risk, and compliance (GRC) and business process automation (BPA). Popular especially in France.
Nimbus Control Nimbus Partners	Captures business process maps and offers collaborative content review; people-centric.
ProVision Metastorm	Links to BPA and BPM suites; easy to use; broad modeling functionality.
QualiWare Product Suite QualiWare	Includes other enterprise architecture capabilities, such as BPA and GRC. Emphasizes collaborative reuse and employee engagement.

Using the Right Tool for the Job

Because they are used commonly for documenting workflows and processes, drawing tools or functions within common business productivity applications, such as PowerPoint or Visio, are often confused with process modeling and repository tools. But such applications only represent relationships, frozen in place at a point in time, in high-level graphics. Little more than a collection of pictures, presentation applications are not dynamically updatable or searchable and are very difficult to propagate among a group of people who need to use them. They are also difficult to maintain and do not effectively support large models.

Why Drawings Are Not Enough

A repository and modeling tool is very different from a drawing tool. Many companies think that they can use PowerPoint or Visio as their repository tool. In 2010 we introduced the Process of Process Management at an organization. The head of one business unit said, "OK, we can skip this repository step; we already have a repository." He put a tall stack of Visio diagrams in front of us. "Here is our repository. We have everything nicely stored. That's all we need." We said, "That's a great start. Now we want to do a system consolidation using the PoPM. Can you tell us which processes are affected by your inventory system?" He said, "No problem; I will ask my assistant to go through those flowcharts. He'll get back to you tomorrow afternoon." We said, "That's great. Now which processes involve your sales department?" He said, "OK, I can ask him to look for the sales department and make a list." And then we said, "And we need to know where you deal with customer master data." Then he looked at his pile and said, "OK, I get your point. Maybe it's not sufficient just to have drawings and other process-related information."

The big difference with a repository tool is that you don't just have drawings; you have dynamic information around processes. That means you have functions, organizational units, and system information, all interrelated so that you can display it graphically to get transparency and also get very specific information out of it. Further, if you make changes in one place, they propagate other areas, helping you keep all the models up to date.

A true repository tool will be easy to maintain; be consistent across models; and have internal governance to enforce modeling methods and disallow "renegade" model types.

In a process modeling and repository tool, practitioners produce and store models in a dynamic environment, which generates reports, details departments involved in specific processes, describes dependencies on databases and master data, and so on. Process modeling and repository tools contain dynamic information around processes. For instance, if a department changes its name, the centralized database propagates that information across all the diagrams and relationships stored in the system.

> Prior to Accenture's move to a repository tool about five years ago, we also used PowerPoint and Visio for our reference models. We didn't realize how much time was wasted on reworking the drawings until we switched to a repository tool. The pace of new model development suddenly accelerated and more time was available for new work, which had been spent on maintaining existing models.

Process modeling and repository tools capture all the elements of a process, including functions, organizational units, and system information, whose relationships are displayed in an integrated, transparent fashion.

One of the preeminent tools for process modeling and repositories is the ARIS Toolset. A brief look at the history of process modeling, which led to the creation of this tool, is instructive. In the late 1980s, August-Wilhelm Scheer recognized that the preponderance of process models meant that no organization could get a clear grasp of all its processes by simply looking at them on a piece of paper. He also recognized that using standard graphical drawing tools would result in chaos. He began to research and develop an architecture for modeling processes, since existing architectures had gaps. He called it the Architecture of Integrated Information Systems, or ARIS.[2] It is perhaps unfortunate that he used the same name to describe the more focused modeling toolset, as this leads to some confusion. Scheer's thoughts on the broader architecture are widely accepted as a good reference framework.

Scheer stated that a business process can be described from five different points of view, which answer all relevant questions regarding a process:

* *Organization view:* Who (people, departments, enterprises, etc.) is involved in the process?
* *Function view:* What functions are carried out during the process?
* *Data view:* What data (information) is needed or produced in the process?
* *Deliverable view:* What are the deliverables of the process? Why do I need them?
* *Control view:* How do all those views fit together?
  o Who is doing what?
  o By means of which data?
  o To produce which deliverables?
  o In which logical sequence are the functions carried out?

This architecture, along with questions it answers, is shown in Figure 7-1.

The central element of ARIS is the control view. It shows how aspects of a process fit together; for example, who is responsible or accountable for a specific function (the organization and function views) or which function uses certain data (the function and data views). The resulting integrated view of various aspects of a business process is the key to successful management of the process and

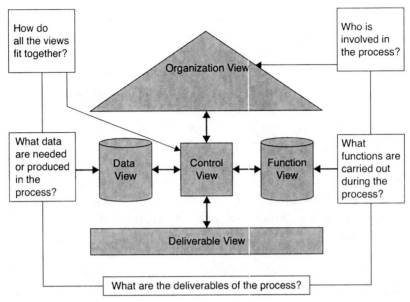

FIGURE 7-1. The ARIS Architecture

is essential for value-driven BPM. The integrated view captured in models such as ARIS enables value-driven BPM's comprehensive approach.

Using the ARIS framework, we can describe exchanges between or within companies. There may be a shift of organizational units from one organization to the other, a reallocation of functions or deliverables, an exchange of data, or a change of control activities between companies.

If a practitioner can answer the "ARIS questions," a business process is sufficiently described to drive a business transformation, minor continuous improvement, or any action that can improve processes.

Examples of business processes include the order-to-cash process, from the time a customer order enters an enterprise until the required products are delivered and paid; a maintenance process, from the time the maintenance order is created until the equipment is maintained; or a hiring process, from the time the hiring request is submitted until the employee is on board. These are operational processes; in other words, their focus is on executing the operational tasks of a company.

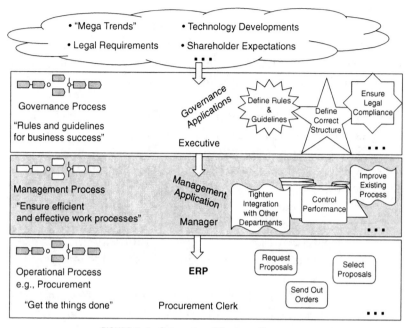

FIGURE 7-2. Categories of Business Processes

(From Mathias Kirchmer, *High Performance Through Process Excellence*, 2nd ed., Berlin: Springer-Verlag, 2011)

Every organization also needs management processes, which ensure the efficient and effective organization of the operational processes. Examples include the evaluation of employee performance or the process of managing a company's IT support. The Process of Process Management, which underpins value-driven BPM, is itself a management process.

Finally, organizations need governance, overall rules and guidelines. In one example, those processes enforce compliance with legal regulations, general megatrends, technological developments, and shareholder expectations. The three types of processes are illustrated in Figure 7-2.

After perfecting the ARIS concept, Scheer then attempted to sell the idea to some of the large IT vendors. Unable to raise interest from other vendors, he then founded his own company, IDS Scheer AG, and began to market the tool. The company grew to more than 3,000 employees before it merged with Software AG in 2009.

Benefits of Process Repositories

Since we are often asked why modeling and repository tools should be used, here's a brief look at their benefits. The key strategic benefits of a process repository derive from the transparency that the repository offers. Process repositories provide these benefits:

- A basis for standardization of selected processes, including cost savings from leveraging best practices and making standard processes more efficient
- A tool to control the degree of process centralization, achieving cost savings through shared service centers and reconciling customer-service orientation with back-office efficiency
- Transparency to support process transformation, which can form the basis for innovation initiatives and focused process improvements
- A basis for setting the scope of software implementation projects, including the definition of software requirements and the management of functional gaps and overlaps
- A basis for a process governance approach

One example of a company gaining strategic benefit from a repository is the high-tech firm discussed in Chapter 3 (and described in more detail in Case Study 2 in Chapter 9). In that case, the repository provided needed transparency into the processes so that the company could focus its investment and scale up its engineering and production processes. Had the company failed to implement a repository, there would have been a high risk of misallocating funds toward nonproductive projects.

Lack of transparency has a negative effect. A machinery company's executives were very proud that they had been able to automate the final assembly line with some industry-leading automation technology. Six months later, there was still little bottom-line benefit. The company had zealously accelerated its assembly line without first pinpointing flaws in the end-to-end process. In this case, poor master data meant that parts went missing because of poor requirements planning. Final assembly continued to run behind schedule. If the company had used a repository, its leaders might have seen the gaps in the process and solved them, instead of automating an already flawed process.

In addition to strategic benefits, process repositories also provide numerous operational benefits:

- Easier use and reuse of process models and model components in design activities
- Easier integration of process models with underlying execution technologies, especially with SOA-based architectures
- Greater flexibility, as model content can be used in various forms (for example, flowcharts to support training as well as text or spreadsheets)
- Protection of process assets, as models can be easily moved from one technical environment into another
- Support of defining process content products that can be sold to other companies or transferred to other divisions
- Consistent process modeling methods and standards within and across industries and functions

BUSINESS PROCESS MANAGEMENT EXECUTION SYSTEMS

Once process knowledge is captured in a repository, a business process management system (BPMS) helps to execute the parts of the process that need automation. A BPMS can automate workflows and facilitate interactive document modification between parties.

There are two main types of BPMS: people-centric and system-centric. People-centric systems route documents through a workflow, and the activities (for example, filling out a purchase request) are carried out by people. System-centric BPMS calls software models to execute functions automatically. This means they include enterprise application integration (EAI) software components to link to applications. Increasingly, BPMS systems include both capabilities.

Practitioners begin working with a BPMS at a simple level, such as passing a document for approvals. Here, the main emphasis is on capturing workflow logic. The advantage of doing this is transparency, identifying bottlenecks. To achieve a higher degree of automation, BPMS can be integrated with other software through enterprise application integration. Multiple applications may be involved in a process, especially if it touches many departments. The interaction between the workflow and these applications can be automated through EAI under the direction of a BPMS. This can help practitioners gain transparency, efficiency, and better compliance, usually with more agility than might be possible using only ERP.

Table 7-2 provides an illustrative list of some BPMS products. Note that this is not meant to be an exhaustive list, rather a sampling of market leaders as well as some emerging players.

TABLE 7-2. A Sampling of BPMS Products

Company/Product	Description
Appian Enterprise	User-friendly, strong in mobile and social BPM with a tightly integrated environment covering process design, execution, management and optimization, analytics, and collaboration.
Cordys Business Operations Platform	Composition-based user interface, with master data management, case management templates, and repository views and access—one of the few natively cloud-enabled platforms. Horizontal offerings include Lean Six Sigma, human-centric workflow, and cloud provisioning. Verticals include financial services, energy and utilities, and manufacturing.[1]
IBM WebSphere Lombardi Edition	Automated, model-driven BPM. SaaS-based high-level process diagramming; easy for business users with intuitive process modeling software that meets different users' perspectives; often used for departmental subprocesses.[2]
OpenText Metastorm Business Process Management	Recently acquired by OpenText to complement its Enterprise Content Management offering, Metastorm supports the process-improvement life cycle. Easy for nontechnical users; extends and leverages Microsoft technologies.[3]
Oracle BPM Suite	Comprehensive and integrated BPM suite including complex events processing, business rules, and optimization capabilities. BPMN 2.0 compliant. Oracle BPM Suite is now the core process platform for Oracle applications.
Pegasystems PRPC	Unified object architecture for all process artifacts (processes, rules, user interfaces) that ease maintainability; supports social networking, role-based tools; heavily focused on financial services and health care;[4] many prebuilt templates to accelerate application building.
Software AG webMethods	Highly integrated with its SOA technologies; user interface based on Eclipse appropriate for IT users; leading the modeling to execution round-trip with a tight integration with the ARIS process modeling tools.[5]

1. Maureen Fleming and Jeff Silverstein, "IDC MarketScape: Worldwide Business Process Platforms 2011 Vendor Analysis," Framingham, MA, 2011.

2-5. Jim Sinur and Janelle B. Hill, "Magic Quadrant for Business Process Management Suites," Gartner, Stamford, CT, 2010.

Recently, BPMS can be accessed through the cloud, a delivery method sometimes referred to as platform as a service (PaaS).

BPMS at a Large Global Bank

A global bank set out to establish an offshore Center of Excellence in the Philippines, where a substantial amount of its back-office finance processes were housed. Given the scale and scope of the bank's global operations, the CoE creation process was a large undertaking. The bank needed value-driven BPM to integrate the wide range of finance processes under one umbrella. Accenture helped the bank optimize, simplify, and standardize finance processes as well as implement a greater degree of automation by integrating Intalio, an open-source BPM product, with existing SAP ERP systems. Now, the bank has real-time process performance visibility through a dashboard for team leaders and senior management. This provides for more balanced workloads and a better ability to anticipate process bottlenecks and backlogs, increasing efficiency, boosting client satisfaction, and enhancing regulatory compliance—top values that led to the creation of the CoE in the first place.

Key to successful automation of processes is the definition and management of business rules. An example business rule is "Department heads must approve purchase requisitions over $1,000." Most organizations have thousands of such rules, which can be managed and executed through business rules engines. Such rules engines need to be integrated into the BPMS to achieve effective automation, especially of more complex processes.

Although it may be tempting, we don't recommend using the graphical design features of a BPMS system to replace the functions of a process modeling and repository tool. Generally, BPMS graphical modeling functions are sufficient only to support tasks that the BPMS software can perform itself. The graphical features are not sufficient to model the entire enterprise. A BPMS is not the optimal tool for creating an enterprise repository because it does not encompass the entirety of the business architecture. Content should be loaded from the enterprise repository into the BPMS repository, establishing a hierarchy of repositories, with the enterprise repository at the highest level.

THE ROLE OF SERVICE-ORIENTED ARCHITECTURE _____

Service-oriented architecture (SOA) has gained currency in the IT world because it provides flexibility for incorporating custom process design into software and essentially separates process design from IT support. Unlike an ERP system, which is typically so fully featured that it has its own set of processes, SOA allows composite applications to be created that can provide exactly what business processes require. SOAs enable separation of business process design and support through appropriate software applications or through application components delivered as services.[3]

Whatever the technical implementation, SOA is in some ways the ideal platform for supporting the goals of agility and innovation held by value-driven BPM. Instead of engineering complex program-to-program interfaces, as required when creating ERP add-ons, all software components are simply linked directly into the integration environment of the SOA. Thus, the connection between process design and execution is more explicit and immediate.

The other main advantage of SOAs over traditional software is that traditional software systems embed only common, widely used processes. Commercial software developers find it financially advantageous to support the broadest possible groups by embedding the most common processes. The result of these embedded processes is that users may design their processes around the software, instead of adapting the software to the processes. This is actually a benefit for the 80 to 85 percent of standard processes that every enterprise performs and from which they gain no specific advantage (think payroll) since the software embeds collective learning from thousands of implementations. But for the 15 to 20 percent of processes that truly differentiate a company, the processes baked into standard systems are not optimal. Key value-driving processes are often custom processes or could be sourced from the cloud.

SOAs have advantages for value-driven BPM because they are easier to configure based on process models in the repository. Practitioners can create an automated process that is precisely consistent with the needs of the organization. Services call applications at every step of the process. Such a design can support the addition or alteration of new services relatively easily. Figure 7-3 shows what such an architecture looks like.

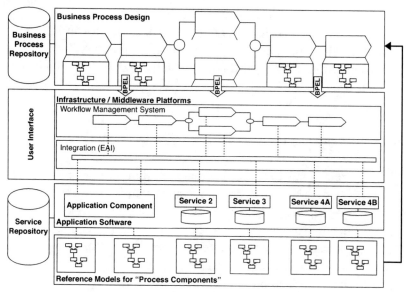

FIGURE 7-3. Service-Oriented Architecture

(From Mathias Kirchmer, High Performance Through Process Excellence, 2nd ed., Berlin: Springer-Verlag, 2011)

The disadvantage of SOAs is their high degree of freedom, which needs to be managed, creating more responsibilities within the organization. It is not advisable to try to structure a highly commoditized process this way because it takes more effort to get the same results that a standard ERP implementation delivers. And, like other solutions, SOAs do not offer much advantage if they are not fed by a structured process model.

There is considerable misunderstanding about SOA among process designers. Many companies believe that they have an SOA, but what they may actually have instead is an EAI linking very traditional systems that still dictate process to the owners, rather than the other way around. Nevertheless, an SOA is not a silver bullet for creating outside-the-box processes. It is not safe to assume that each transaction in a process design will be represented, one-for-one, by an analogous transaction in an execution system. Custom design work is still required to make SOAs function for BPM objectives.

Organizations get the most strategic benefit from an SOA when it is part of the overall BPM environment—in other words, when it is actually used to drive innovation and agility and becomes the compelling force behind value-driven BPM agendas. If the SOA is solely used to cut costs for IT and the organization goes on with business as usual, you're missing an opportunity. Value-driven BPM as a management discipline gets the most value out of SOA and the flexibility it provides.

PROCESS PERFORMANCE MONITORING SYSTEMS

Once a process has been designed and set in motion, practitioners need to investigate its performance against standards for operational quality, service levels, and cost, among many other factors. The feedback from such process performance monitoring systems (PPMS) can then be used as information to optimize the process through the life-cycle phases of value-driven BPM.

Traditional process monitoring systems come in two flavors:

- IT-centric systems measure computer uptime, downtime, and performance and are primarily concerned with technological assets that support processes.
- Classical analytic systems typically explore cost performance in cost centers, or information about the performance of a certain department, but provide no clear picture of an end-to-end process as it crosses multiple departments. Such systems fall into two categories. Some perform analysis in real time while others can only perform analysis of data after the process has been executed. It's important to know which type best meets your needs. Typical examples are analytic functionality of ERP systems or accounting applications.

Additionally, business process execution and automation tools do contain some performance monitoring capabilities. To close the gap between BPMS and traditional process monitoring systems, the process performance monitoring system was born. A PPMS monitors key performance indicators of processes and delivers other contextual information so that practitioners have all the information they need to control and adjust processes. Through a defined, low-level view of inputs and outputs of software that supports processes in the organization, a PPMS can systematically gather qualitative and quantitative data, allowing practitioners to perform analysis.

As with traditional process monitoring systems, there are two types of PPMS: real-time monitoring, which helps avoid problems while the process is under way; and process analytics, based on historical data, which allows practitioners to see trends and act on them.

Process Mining: The Next Step in BPM Technology

Process mining is an advanced technique for discovering the execution of processes. Process mining reverse-engineers the process models of subprocesses that are automated (ERP, BPMS, etc.).[4]

Process mining goes so far as to probe the system logs of transactional systems, providing a detailed account of where processes break down or could function better, and relates these to standard KPIs. Process mining can show how long someone worked on a document or trace a sales order across multiple systems, including the time stamps marking when the order left one system and entered another. This means that a formerly chin-scratching question such as "Why is the sales cycle increasing?" can be answered much more easily. Process mining can locate the top orders with the longest sales cycle times and examine them for bottlenecks.

One ideal use case for PPMS might involve processes that are opaque and locked inside an enterprise system but that could be strategically important. A PPMS allows practitioners to model processes and infuse them with more reporting and data, giving greater insight than simply jumping from modeling to execution. With PPMS and process mining, practitioners can get information about processes, enabling faster and better understanding. For instance, the roadmap creation process can be informed by both high-level, strategic planning information as well as granular, ground-level information—practitioners can determine how much a process is costing them in the aggregate, over years, as a market strategy, as well as in shorter bursts and at greater levels of detail.

In essence, with PPMS, process modeling is connected to reporting and data that affords great insight—and transparency—into how to make process execution work better. It delivers real "process KPIs," such as frequencies, cycle times, and the like. Using a PPMS and process mining capability at a Loyalty Card company, we discovered that the performance of the call center had been very bad in February over several years (we used historic data as input). The first reaction of the company was that there must be a bug in the PPMS. But after analysis of the business situation, it discovered that it had an issue with its vacation policy: since people had to use all "old" vacation time before the first of March (or lose it), many decided to take the last days off in February—leading to the performance issues that month.

THE PROMISE OF ENTERPRISE 2.0 AND SOCIAL MEDIA ____

People are key for value-driven BPM, so the use of social media and Web 2.0 can be an important enabler of value-driven BPM. Social media provide a bridge between IT and people and close the gap between process design and the design of systems to support process. IT becomes less of a bottleneck as a result. Social media can be used to support the development of the culture we discussed in Chapter 6.

A quick look across the office will likely reveal Facebook or YouTube open on someone's desktop. While this might seem to be a preamble to an argument about increasing security and locking down firewalls, in fact it is quite the opposite. The corporate office is now part of Enterprise 2.0—companies now use social media for business purposes. It can lead to agility, innovation, internal integration, and the creative use of networks.

Nimble, lightweight applications delivered over the web as services could be the primary mode of delivering business value in the future. The ability of the web to socialize business activity within and between organizations has become instrumental to squeezing more value out of processes and creating entirely new processes, and this influence will doubtless continue to grow. Social media can now be used to support the Process of Process Management and value-driven BPM as a management discipline as well as to execute or support operational processes. These aspects are often discussed as "social BPM."

A key differentiator of any Web 2.0 service or application is that the more people use it, the more it improves in both results and usefulness. Therefore, such an application either solicits data directly from the user or finds intelligent data-mining capabilities to continuously produce better data. Examples of such Web 2.0 applications include Wikipedia, created and maintained by its users; social networks such as LinkedIn; and Google, which improves search results based on characteristics of past searches. Web 2.0 applications often utilize mash-ups that take data from existing web applications and combine them with new content, delivering additional value to the user without changing the original sources. This can be helpful in implementing and maintaining a culture of value-driven BPM. For example, the senior vice president of strategy at a major retail chain introduces a social media platform as part of his value-driven BPM initiative. A blog from the CEO reaffirms the culture requirement and demonstrates the top-down mandate.

Enterprise 2.0

Although many Web 2.0 applications are focused on private users, many initiatives exist to transfer those capabilities into the business world, targeting enterprise clients. This is Enterprise 2.0: the phenomenon of a company using the capabilities of Web 2.0 for its business purposes, including its business-to-business environment. As an example, Accenture has an internal social media application supported by a comprehensive Knowledge Exchange, which uses wikis and blogs to introduce new tools and concepts and allows contributors to quickly generate and receive feedback in an iterative and widely distributed fashion. These new web capabilities require an appropriate management approach.

This new approach to management will in many ways revolve around adaptations to traditional process design and governance to accommodate and capitalize on Enterprise 2.0. Questions that should be asked of the process champions in an organization include the following:

- How can organizations encourage people to put their ideas in shareable process models, yet make sure that process model development is still targeted and drives the organization in one direction?
- How can innovation be encouraged while avoiding the introduction of risk?
- What governance models might apply?
- Can the Wikipedia model—where a form of community policing results in corrections and the removal of self-serving information—be used within the enterprise for a process repository, for instance?

- How can governance be developed such that the process repository is continuously improved, but with discipline and direction?

What might the "Enterprise 2.0+," social-media, value-driven BPM organization look like? A look at the IT architecture inside Enterprise 2.0 is shown in Figure 7-4. The core of this Enterprise 2.0+ approach is an SOA environment integrated with one BPM engine for design and implementation and another integrated component for the management and control of the executed business processes. Similar in concept to an SOA, some processes are triggered by specific external events, resulting in an event-driven SOA. This real-time event management is also reflected in the BPM software.

Quality issues in delivered materials may immediately trigger quality assurance processes, or the arrival of a specific customer order type may lead to certain order-handling activities. Extraordinary events, such as extreme cycle times for an order, may lead to corrective activities related to the specific situation. Generally, real-time reactions can happen in response to real-time events. Master data management is handled across operational processes to avoid redundancies and inconsistencies. The "internet of things"—the vast network of connected, "smart" IT and non-IT devices—will play an increasing role in process design as well as active management of a far-flung universe of assets, accessed through dashboards and other graphical tools that allow quick, at-a-glance information and responses.

Other New Developments

The BPM design component can receive external input through the web. This may include general experiences regarding certain business issues, or formal reference models showing relevant business practices. In return, an enterprise also provides this information to others. BPM event management also reacts to external events, such as price changes for raw materials, or general macroeconomic events, such as changes in currency exchange rates. The SOA may not only use internal software components but also support business processes through application services delivered via the Internet. It may even power itself through the web via platform as a service.

Software as a service (SaaS) takes this concept one step further by "renting" services to users, and it is already the preferred mode of

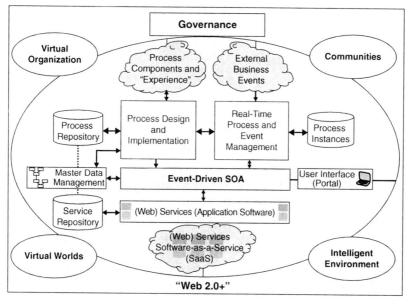

FIGURE 7-4. Enterprise 2.0+ integrated with the Business Environment

(From Mathias Kirchmer, High-Performance Through Process Excellence, 2nd ed., Berlin: Springer-Verlag, 2011)

delivery for many internal and external software customers. Cloud computing will have a similar effect on agility and efficiency because it separates processes from the hardware that supports them, giving organizations more flexibility to leverage key assets within and outside their own four walls.

Enterprise 2.0+

Enterprise 2.0+ identifies an organization wherein Web 2.0+ is no longer a nebulous concept on the fringe of the universe. Instead, Web 2.0+ is highly integrated with the business environment, as shown in Figure 7-4.

A company may be a member of many online communities. Imagine using an environment like YouTube to exchange business process models and narrated presentations. Instead of just posting videos, companies could post process models representing their best business practices or other interesting process ideas. This could facilitate the exchange of business experiences within and across industries.[5]

Enterprise 2.0+ could not only become part of a powerful virtual organization but also create value networks that extend far beyond a single organization. For example, one could create an innovation network around the company, including customers, partners, research institutes, universities, and other entities that would benefit from collaborating on a given set of ideas. This could be extended even further to other organizations. The exchange of ideas could be organized through blogs and other prevalent social media devices, such as Twitter-like business applications.

Social media may yet be one of the strongest enablers of value-driven BPM. For example, in the effort to build up the process organization, companies can use community-building software or blogs to solicit input from stakeholders, and use this capability as a vital building block of the BPM community (part of the PoPM). The use of social media for a collaborative process design could be another component of value-driven BPM.

Additionally, social media can be used to improve operational processes. For example, workflow software could trigger a blog post when certain events occur, such as a delivery with poor material quality. The various owners of, and experts connected to, that process would be notified on their mobile devices and computers. In no time, practitioners around the world could begin diagnosing the problem and developing a workaround in a traceable forum, capturing the knowledge from the blog and populating it into BPM-related systems.

The Intelligent Environment

Until now, the standard method for loading data into enterprise systems has been through manual entry. This is often very costly and leads to delays. Auto-identification technologies such as radio frequency identification (RFID) enable the automated creation of data. For example, once containers are loaded into a ship, this information is automatically transferred through RFID into a software system, and from there it becomes available through the web.

The result is an "intelligent environment" or the "internet of things," referred to above, which ultimately leads to business processes that enable high performance. But similar technologies can also be used to improve products and services, creating "intelligent products" that behave in a context-sensitive way, such as driverless cars that brake whenever obstacles are detected.[6]

This intelligent environment incrementally closes the gap between the real and the virtual world. Once more and more information about the real world is digitized, this information can be used as building blocks for a virtual world, allowing the realistic testing and validation of new business processes and removing from product development some of the risk of running process simulations that ultimately represent reality only so well. The boundaries between the real and virtual worlds have already begun to blur.

In business, this means that the gaps between agility, efficiency, and quality shrink, because transparency is increasing.

Perhaps the key challenge of Enterprise 2.0+ is not perfecting technology but finding the appropriate governance model. This is what a good PoPM provides. Here Enterprise 2.0+ is part of an overall value-driven BPM discipline. Web 2.0+ empowers people and encourages creativity. But how can companies ensure that employees will still work toward the company's goals? A traditional governance model, consisting of many inflexible rules and policies, does not work in such an environment (see Chapter 6). The Wikipedia model could apply, but enterprises are more complex than knowledge communities such as Wikipedia, and incorrect information could be far more harmful. Nevertheless, Web 2.0+ communities point the way to the future of process design and implementation.

Enterprise 2.0+ is clearly a perfect environment for value-driven BPM, because it is a huge step forward in terms of transparency, which is the vital ingredient of value-driven BPM. It permanently delivers the information necessary for timely decisions and supports the near real-time execution of the resulting actions. As a result, strategy and operational performance are closely integrated.

Perhaps more than any single technology, the transparency introduced by Enterprise 2.0+ brings the value framework into crisp reality for practitioners. Organizations can both be more efficient and achieve better-quality work. They will be able to accomplish these goals with agility, even while operating at a higher level of compliance with regulations than before. Networking and integration actually go hand in hand when open, extensible technology is underlain by sophisticated role and permission controls.[7]

Ultimately, high performance, as well as the success of value-driven BPM, depends on people and the way they act within their business processes. Before its promise can be delivered, Enterprise 2.0+ needs to be accepted by people, who will always be the most important factor in a high-performance organization. They need to understand how Enterprise 2.0+ will elevate the entire organization and the ecosystem around it and recognize the validation that will come to them from the role they and their peers will play in setting a foundation for unprecedented innovation.

Notes

1. Chris Wilson and Julie Short, "Magic Quadrant for Enterprise Architecture Tools," Gartner, Stamford, CT, October 28, 2010.

2. August-Wilhelm Scheer, *ARIS: Business Process Frameworks*, 3rd ed. (Berlin: Springer-Verlag, 2000).

3. Mathias Kirchmer, *High-Performance Through Process Excellence,* 2nd ed. (Berlin: Springer-Verlag, 2011).

4. Mathias Kirchmer, Francisco Gutierrez, and Sigifredo Laengle, "Process Mining for Organizational Agility," *Industrial Management*, January/February 2010.

5. Mathias Kirchmer, *High-Performance Through Process Excellence,* 2nd ed. (Berlin: Springer-Verlag, 2011).

6. Elgar Fleisch, Oliver Christ, and Markus Dierkes, "Die betriebswirtschaftliche Vision des Internets der Dinge." In *Das Internet der Dinge: Ubiquitous Computing und RFID in der Praxis*, ed. Elgar Fleisch and Friedemann Mattern (Springer-Verlag: Berlin, 2005), 3–37.

7. Peter Franz, Mathias Kirchmer, and Michael Rosemann, "Value-Driven Business Process Management: Which Values Matter for BPM," Accenture and Queensland University of Technology, 2011.

CHAPTER 8

Managing Information Models for Value-Driven BPM

Process models are the heart of business process management. The way that a company works, or the way that it intends to work, is typically captured in models that can be used for communication, education, design, automation, and many other purposes. To master the management discipline of value-driven BPM, it is vital to have a clear understanding of what a process model is and how a process repository can help create, manage, and raise awareness of models. In this chapter, we shift to the issue of content and content management and examine the ways that process models are created and managed.

In a sense, the art of creating and managing process models is a special form of content management. The models themselves are the content. The repository is a vehicle for managing and delivering the content, just as printed pages, a Kindle, or an iPad all can be the vehicle to publish the same book. Of course, in the case of a process model, the content is alive and changing, and it should be updated as needed and delivered in many different forms to different audiences.

Creating and curating the right content and choosing and using the right vehicle are essential to obtaining the desired value from the technology and from BPM in general. Many companies make substantial investments in tools that go underutilized or unused because of a lack of substantive process content. We discuss why it's important to create content in the form of process models and business architectures, and we discuss use cases for repositories as well as repository strategies and success factors. We address such questions as, "How are process models used?" and "How can they become assets that drive value?" The view of such content as assets is key: knowledge is transferred in the form of process models and business architectures, which are managed in such a way that they can be continuously used and reused, providing more and more value.

This chapter continues with a discussion of how organizations can jump-start their content building and process management with the use of a specialized form of content known as reference models, which are templates for standard forms of processes that can be adapted to organization-specific requirements. These models include process models and libraries but can also include value components such as KPI frameworks, value trees, process impact matrices, and more.

We conclude the chapter with a discussion of the advantages of using reference models, and, through the use of examples, we examine how and when reference models can be used to create the most value. This chapter incorporates the insights from one aspect of our research into how successful organizations have received practical value out of such reference models and frameworks. We also discuss a new, upcoming market for reference models.

WHY YOU NEED PROCESS MODELS AND REPOSITORIES ⎯⎯

With the rise in the 1990s of Scheer's ARIS architecture, the Zachman Framework, and the U.S. Department of Defense Architecture Framework (DODAF), the market began to fill with process frameworks.[1] The tools for storing and deploying these models also entered the market, in the form of Scheer's ARIS Toolset, Provision, Casewise, Nimbus, System Architect, and many others, as described in Chapter 7. Tools became easier to use and more broadly accepted. People rushed to build models of their processes, and suddenly organizations had many repositories, but too often, no one looked at them. People had modeled for modeling's sake, without any context or perspective about why they were modeling. The models were exceedingly complex and had been built under the mistaken impression that buying a repository product and building models was the equivalent of developing a BPM capability.

Repositories are important, but the true rewards come from a value-driven approach to building and *using* process models. This means understanding the use case for these tools at some level of detail, understanding that the implementation should have proper governance and ownership within the organization, and understanding that, despite quantum leaps in the power of software, there is still quite a lot of human legwork, comprehension, and commitment involved in making tools work effectively within the organization and with its partners. In other words, a repository without a Process of Process Management (PoPM) implemented as described in this book seldom leads to significant business value. A repository used with a PoPM can be a powerful tool for effecting change and optimizing processes at all levels of a company. In this chapter, we explain the rationale behind process models and repositories, suggest critical success factors for using repositories, and provide guidance on how to find good examples.

Process models and repositories are nothing new. They have been around since the early days of the Industrial Revolution in the form of routings and bills of material. Today, process models are highly sophisticated, as is the software that supports them. Process models and repositories capture the accumulated knowledge of generations of workers and offer efficiency in modifying processes or creating new ones. Process models provide a structured, formal description of processes, while repositories store and manage process models in an organized fashion for easy retrieval and reuse. Process models are the master data of value-driven BPM, and we use the Process of Process Management to implement them.

Drivers for Process Modeling and Repositories

CHANGING BUSINESS ENVIRONMENT

Frequently changing operating models: How can an organization keep track of changes to operating models in one division that may affect the processes and ability to change in another division?

Mergers and acquisitions: When one company acquires another, how can the combined companies accelerate the synergies that drove the merger in the first place? It is much easier to consolidate processes when they are well understood and documented.

Globalization and new markets: Expanding into new markets requires a quick assimilation of new regulations, customs, trade laws, and other procedures, all of which require the ability to quickly model, alter, merge, and store processes.

Global supply chains: Increasingly, ecosystems are only as good as their supply chains. As partners are added or changed, the ability to quickly adapt and integrate their processes into the workflow of the organization represents a competitive advantage—a connection to value.

Product and process innovation: Modeling and documenting a process can reveal inefficiencies. The ability to remove kinks in the process can help accelerate the life cycle of product development or production processes.

Faster time-to-market: A shareable, collaborative model with reusable parts lets a far-flung, cross-disciplinary team create products and bring them to market faster.

Cost pressure from increased competition: Organizations are under intense pressure to innovate and develop new products and processes while containing costs. A process repository reconciles information about what has been done before and worked well, or not so well, and its visual capabilities enable faster decisions that drive improved efficiency and new outcomes.

CHANGING TECHNOLOGY

New technologies: Business user-focused technologies close the gap between process design and execution and require much less IT support while increasing the need for robust, accurate, and reliable process models.

New concepts: Model-driven software development doesn't work without well-constructed process models.

CHANGING SOCIOECONOMIC ENVIRONMENT

Aging workforce: The experience of workers needs to be captured in process assets before they retire and their deep knowledge walks out the door.

Informed and demanding customers: Why can't you find out about a missing shipment as quickly as you can find an address on Google Maps? Organizations increasingly need to support quick responses; processes should be tightly integrated to provide those answers.

Uses of Repositories

In this chapter we are primarily focused on the content of repositories—process models—as opposed to the tools (software) that allow repositories to operate (see Chapter 7). Here, we are looking at the logical arrangement of repositories as storehouses of process model content, rather than as software products.

A repository is an environment for storing, retrieving, and reusing process models. Process models help codify how a company does things in a way that can be referenced and changed when needed. Repositories contain best practices and process models that can represent years of innovation and process improvement. When a process needs to be created or revised, accessing the models gives practitioners a foundation from which to begin, helping them to avoid reinventing the wheel. But, of course, this only happens if a PoPM and process culture is in place. Then people are aware that the repository exists, want to use it as part of doing their jobs, and know that it contains valuable information that can help them.

Transparency is at the heart of value-driven BPM, as described in Chapters 1 and 2. A repository, properly structured, provides this transparency. The target audiences, primary use cases, and benefits of repositories are detailed in Table 8-1.

TABLE 8-1. Use Cases for Repositories

Audience	Use Case	Benefits
Members of affected business audience	Rolling out strategic changes, such as business transformations or translating a new operating model into executable steps	Operationalization of change, transparency over what to do
Affected business units, IT owner of ERP models	Driving the implementation of large applications, such as ERP	Transparency over business content of ERP system and new to-be processes; focus on business outcomes of ERP implementation
Process owner, business	Defining measurement points for KPIs/Metrics	End-to-end process visibility
Executives who set business strategy	Supporting innovation around new processes	Simulations to try out processes; transparency over impacts
Affected business units, compliance department	Enhancing or enabling compliance	Exact definition of required working steps; integration of procedures in daily processes; transparency; required documentation
Business, IT	Capturing knowledge for training and education	Transfer of knowledge into reusable assets, foster onboarding of new people; reduce dependency on key know-how people

(continued)

TABLE 8-1. Use Cases for Repositories, *continued*

Audience	Use Case	Benefits
HR, affected business units	Creating job descriptions by accurately diagramming all the tasks involved	Customer/market focus through integration of jobs into end-to-end processes
Risk department, affected business units	Improving risk management	Integrate risk management system directly into day-to-day processes
IT	Consolidating applications	Reduction of risk of negative business impact, opportunity to provide business improvement
All affected business units	Facilitating process improvement	Business-wide benefits
IT, Finance	Driving process-oriented system consolidation	Simplified system landscape
Business, IT	Bridging the gap between BPM models for software development	Software is developed more quickly and better meets business needs; clearer communication around requirements
Compliance department	Enhancing or enabling compliance	Processes are repeatable, and compliance can be baked in

The key to creating a repository for value-driven BPM comes from a clear understanding of why the repository is being created. It is not necessary to have detailed models in all cases. Detail should be included only with a clear outcome in mind.

THE FIVE CRITICAL COMPONENTS OF A REPOSITORY STRATEGY

The classic pitfall of repositories is skipping or only partially fulfilling one of the five critical components that follow (Figure 8-1). To get the most out of the system, you'll need to answer some basic questions, the most important of which is, "Why are we doing this?" It is possible to implement every aspect of a repository perfectly and still get substandard results if there is no clear use case.

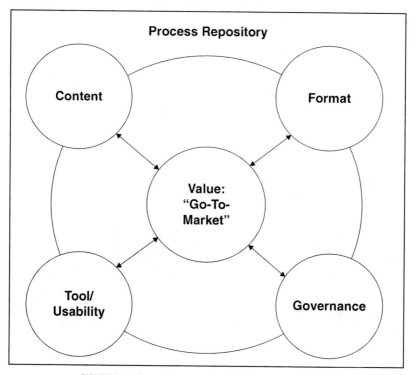

FIGURE 8-1. Crucial Components of a Repository Strategy

In the following sections, we delve into each of the five key elements of a good repository strategy, and present questions to ask how these elements are built into the repository.

Go-to-Market: What Is the Use Case?

Many modeling efforts unravel because practitioners do not define objectives before beginning. In essence, before starting out, the practitioner should answer the following question: "What is the primary value outcome for the model?" Some common primary value outcomes are shown in Table 8-1 earlier in this chapter.

Content: What to Describe

What kind of content is needed to support the use case? The content will depend on the use case. Suppose the use case is risk management. The object here is to study which risks affect the process and how each risk affects the process specifically. Next, you should identify what may be necessary to reduce or mitigate the risk. It's important in this dimension to ask more than one department or department head about risks: a CIO could identify IT risks while a CFO could identify financial risks, for example. Going through this exercise helps ensure that the content of the repository is both valid and useful.

Format: How to Describe the Content

It is certainly possible to document a process entirely in text format. But, given that some processes are very detailed, the document could run into the thousands of pages. It's unlikely that many people will find such a long document useful or appealing. With graphical models, relationships are generally much easier to understand. There are many formats to choose from—there are, for example, more than 200 modeling methods available in the ARIS Toolset alone. Some core modeling methods include the following:

- Event-driven process chain (EPC)
- Business process modeling notation (BPMN)
- Value–added chain diagrams
- Function allocation diagrams
- Entity relationship diagrams
- Function trees
- Organization charts
- Value trees

Each of these has numerous variants—which is both an advantage and a disadvantage. A modeling effort can quickly spin out of control because practitioners become enthusiastic when they find a model that precisely fits their situation.

We recommend deploying as simple and easy-to-use a format as possible. For example, after an initial flurry of interest in more than 50 modeling methods, Accenture was able to cover its entire content landscape with fewer than 10 modeling methods in its internal repository. Focusing on these 10 methods has been critical to achieving the quality and consistency we need in our own processes.

The discipline for limiting modeling to its most effective applications comes from the repository strategy. Governance enforces the outcome.

Governance: How to Control the Development and Maintenance of a Repository

If everyone in the organization is excited about modeling processes, someone, or some part of the organization, needs to take charge of prioritizing which processes need to be modeled and enforce rules around the repository. Standardizing on fewer models in a centralized repository reduces the chaos somewhat, but if everyone in the organization can add his or her models into the repository, chaos returns. To innovate, an organization needs to be capable of accepting new ideas, but there also needs to be a priority system for incorporating them into the repository. Therefore, a hierarchy of permissions and a submission sequence should be established. Here is a sampling of questions to ask at the beginning of the modeling process:

- What is the repository policy when something changes?
- Who identifies whether a process change is necessary?
- Who makes sure process changes are reflected in the repository?
- Who owns the processes and prioritizes when they are released and updated?
- Who can see the repository content?
- Who can modify the repository content?
- Do we have a repository development and production environment? If so, when is the content moved from the development environment to the production environment?
- Who does quality assurance (QA) of the repository?
- How do we measure the success of the repository?

Get the Models Right

As mentioned in the sidebar in Chapter 5 (see page 98), a couple of years ago, we worked with an insurance company that implemented a BPMS and automation system for claims handling, but then noticed that the system only handled two or three of the seven different types of claims the company typically processed. When the company started automating, suddenly it needed people to sort out which claims could go through the automated process, which had to be handled manually, and then bring the results together. This didn't lead to more transparency, agility, or efficiency, but rather to the opposite: it needed more people and more time, and the people made mistakes, so quality went downhill.

Why did this happen? The insurance company did not spend enough time creating its process models. The process models did not cover all the cases and capture the rules. Creating process models involves having policies and standards for creating that content. You need modeling guidelines and conventions. You need governance around changing processes.

Usability and Tools: What Software to Use

Once the use cases, content, format, and governance are defined, practitioners then select the best software tool environment for the repository. Note that we recommend that you define what you want to do first, then find a tool that will support what you want to do, not the other way around. The tendency is to go shopping for a tool and get caught up in tool comparisons before fundamental questions have been asked. Questions to ask include these:

- Which is the best repository tool for us, and which components do we need?
- How do we manage the tool from a technical perspective?
- How can we deploy the tool into the organization?
- How much can we tailor the user interface?
- How easily can we extend or adapt the tool to meet our needs?
- What if any content (reference models) is included?
- Does the tool support a particular methodology, and do we want to use that methodology?

The typical sequence of setting up a tool to support a process model looks like this:

1. Refine use cases
2. Define the content
3. Select the tool
4. Select the format (often driven by the tool's ability to support the format)
5. Establish a system of governance

As with any other process, the use cases for each element of the PoPM need to be properly understood from the user's perspective. The repository is, after all, only a database. Organizations need the right procedures and applications for effectively using this database.

SUCCESS FACTORS FOR A PROCESS REPOSITORY

There are several critical success factors for process repositories, the status of which should be checked periodically during the creation process. First of all, avoid the impulse to do it all—cataloging and modeling every process in the organization at once. As stated earlier, it is much better to focus on critical processes to which identifiable, achievable improvements can be made.

Create Short-Term Wins

Modeling processes can be laborious, and a process-modeling project could fail before completion if fatigue sets in. Setting priorities to create a quick win—the most return for the least effort—can save a project and lay the foundation for more projects.

Make a plan for visible performance improvements that can be achieved by better processes (see Chapter 4), then make those improvements. If the rest of the organization, as well as the process practitioners, can see that the modeling project is successful, it improves acceptance. Employees who participated in the improvements should be recognized and rewarded, showing that process modeling is an important activity. A skeletal but accurate model of a high-impact process is more useful than a highly detailed model of a less-strategic process. More detail can be added to the skeletal model later.

Some Examples of Short-Term Wins

A consumer goods company needed to improve its risk management in a subset of its supply chain. The company modeled only the subprocess affected. That subprocess was modeled in detail and inserted in the overall supply chain model, and a risk manual for the subprocess was generated very quickly.

A telecommunications company implemented a new customer relationship management (CRM) system to support some of its customer-facing processes. The company used product-testing models it developed to implement the CRM system, and then recycled those models into training manuals for the employees.

A global services company implemented a high-level process structure against which it mapped its applications. This structure was used to rationalize IT. Then, it was developed in more detail for processes that needed reengineering, reusing some of the gains made in the earlier effort.

A leading medical technology firm needed to shift from selling medical equipment to services. With this change came longer sales cycles, more intensive presale consultations and configuration, and ongoing service. Working closely with Accenture through a creation process, the firm identified 24 distinct changes, and a short list of actionable, high-payoff projects was created. The changes ultimately selected included revising the auditing process and implementing clearer deadlines. One change had the potential to speed the reimbursement process by a factor of three while reducing administrative costs.

Establish a Sense of Urgency

Before initiating a modeling effort, examine the business and IT issues and opportunities in the company. The most successful process–modeling efforts need to be relevant to pain points that affect the company now. It is common wisdom that people feel pressured to finish projects if they know that their supervisors want them to. Therefore, obtaining executive sponsorship for the modeling effort greatly assists the cause and instills a sense of urgency.

A Holistic, Value-Driven BPM Vision and Strategy

Modeling and repository projects are naturally more successful when connected to outcomes of value, as described in Chapter 4. If you can show a link between improving a process and an outcome of value, it will be easier to define the process modeling and improvement approach, and to achieve buy-in from management and downstream employees.

Well-Defined Framework

Defining the business process repository framework, standards, and guidelines in detail can help keep the project on track. Adherence to strategy needs to be enforced in a systematic way, lest chaos ensue—this is one of the key roles of repository governance. Establishing standards and guidelines includes setting the right filters in the repository to enforce the use of proper formats and methods.

Training and Communication

At the outset of the repository project, assess the need for training and develop a communication plan. Visible performance improvements should be incorporated into the plan because they will promote the success of the project and maximize the impact of the repository. If success stories can be woven into the communication plan, the increased credibility can be used to expand the scope of the project to change other systems, structures, and policies that do not fit the vision expressed by the communication plan.

Integrating the Repository into the Organization

The process repository contains master data about the processes in the organization. Master data needs to be stored in such a way that the entire enterprise can easily access and parse the information, and it should be kept as up-to-date as possible. The repository should be integrated into the infrastructure of the organization so that it supports value-driven BPM in general, and the BPM delivery sub-processes in particular. The people in the organization charged with delivering BPM must learn how to apply the models contained in the repository (see Chapter 3).

The master data needs to be available wherever the organization needs to make a change to a process. Typically, there is an enterprise-wide repository from which select information is loaded into process execution systems. Some of these systems contain their own small repositories that relate directly to the portion of the process the system was designed to execute. These process-execution system repositories need to be fed from the enterprise repository before the process is set in motion.

The repository should be integrated into the infrastructure of the organization and into the training schedule for employees. Computer-based training initiatives should include units on process modeling and repositories.

COMMON MISTAKES IN CREATING
PROCESS REPOSITORIES

These are two common mistakes that we encounter repeatedly in our consultations with organizations that are eager to develop their repository strategies, but don't have a disciplined way of going about it.

Documenting without direction: A consumer-goods company created more than 600 models based on 43 modeling methods. Only one user looked at the repository over the course of a month. From a practical standpoint, the team had created far too many models, at far too high a level of complexity, to be useful. Similarly, a commodity-goods company had a team of 12 people working full time to model its HR processes, and spent six months creating hundreds of models. There was no clear use case, and the governance was unclear. The company was forced to start over because the leaders had not considered what the models would be used for, and, during the extended time period devoted to modeling, the business circumstances being modeled had changed.

Using the wrong tool: Many organizations substitute a drawing tool such as Microsoft Visio for a process-modeling tool in the interest of saving money or avoiding the learning curve of a new piece of software. The return on investment is usually very poor in these cases because standard business software does not accurately represent process relationships and is very limited in terms of dynamic updating capabilities, change tracking, or collaboration. Further, a large model becomes unwieldy, sometimes literally falling off the page.

REFERENCE MODELS AND WHY YOU NEED THEM

Rather than starting from scratch with repository content, many organizations use reference models as a starting point.

There is some degree of confusion about reference models. Many people believe that a reference model is a locked-down, step-by-step set of instructions for a specific process. In fact, reference models are generic conceptual models that formalize recommended practices for a special domain.[2] They have the following characteristics:[3]

- *Representation of best or common practices:* Reference models provide best practices for doing business.
- *Universal applicability:* Reference models deliver business content well beyond an individual issue. That means they will be used not only for one enterprise but also for wide groups of enterprises in the same industry.
- *Reusability:* Reference models are conceptual frameworks that can easily be reused in many information system projects. They are structured for easy adaptability to company-specific situations.

The value of a reference model is that users benefit from experiences others have already had. Reference models can provide common languages for process elements and can be used to:

- Build information models and repositories
- Train staff
- Plan the scope of projects
- Plan interactions with other companies and industries.

A reference model is *not* an authoritative model or statement of requirements for a certain process. A reference model *is* a catalog of useful processes, general knowledge, and best practices on a certain topic, expressed in a structured format that can easily be used and applied in specific situations.

The reusability of reference models has not been lost on software vendors. Large companies such as Accenture or SAP, and smaller companies such as PMOLink, have begun to "productize" reference models, or parts of reference models, for different industries and applications.

Organizations use reference models for many reasons. Table 8-2 summarizes some of the top reasons cited by organizations surveyed by the American Productivity and Quality Center (APQC).

Improving performance management and metrics is clearly a large motivation; it is cited by 61 percent of those interviewed, as was the definition of key processes requiring cross-functional owners—processes that cross boundaries within the organization (45 percent). According to a joint report by APQC and Accenture, the best reference models, developed over time, include "not only

TABLE 8-2. Motivations for Using a Reference Model (source: APQC)

Answer	Distribution
Performance management and metrics	61%
Definition of key processes requiring cross-functional owners	45%
Content management system/knowledge management	30%
Reorganization/reengineering project, merger, divestiture, etc.	29%
Enterprise process taxonomy—basis for enterprise operations (i.e., embedded in enterprise-wide technology and/or tools)	25%
Compliance with an external standard (e.g., ISO 9001)	17%
Accounting; accounting management system or activity-based costing approach	14%
Not using a framework	12%
Other	20%

simple functional compositions but also valuable content, such as chains of cross-functional processes organized into value streams, key performance indicators/associated benchmarking data, and in some cases, best practices related to functional compositions and top performance."[4]

An excellent example of the value of a reference model comes from a global services company that had been working for more than a year to document the structure of the company in a reliable and comprehensible fashion.

The company had five major divisions, each division relying on its own modeling protocol. Owners in each of the divisions felt strongly about their process models, which represented their way of seeing the world. Work had effectively stopped because of this stalemate.

Introducing a reference model for global services created a neutral point from which to restart the effort. Based on this reference model—a common generic standard for how a global services company should operate that was developed through a study of the industry—the company was able to reach a compromise. The teams were able to speak a common language based on the reference model, rather than having each team arguing that its version was better. Using the enterprise-wide industry model at the highest level, the operating model could be broken down and decomposed to lower levels of work under each division director. Each division's model was then pulled up into the main model. Within months, the company had an enterprise-wide model that could be used for consolidating systems, improving processes, and enhancing collaboration that had previously been difficult because of the siloed divisional structure of the company.

TYPES OF REFERENCE MODELS

Reference models are becoming increasingly targeted and focused for different industries and use cases. The choices are multiplying as an increasing number of more organizations realize the value that is buried in their existing processes and identify room for improvement after observing successes attributable to the process excellence of their competitors in the marketplace. Academics, industry organizations, software companies, and consultancies alike have seen the value of reference models, and, as a result, a wealth of information about reference models is available as well as templates from which to begin to build your own reference model. Listed below are some prominent reference models:

1. *Industry reference models* representing best practices for a specific industry sector, such as banking or consumer packaged goods
   - eTOM (enhanced Telecom Operations Map), published by the TM Forum
   - Accenture business process reference models are available for 71 industries in the following fields:
     - Utility
     - Energy
     - Chemicals and natural resources
     - Banking and insurance

- o Communications
- o Engineering and high-tech
- o Consumer goods and services
- o Health and life science
- o Postal
- o HR
- o The Process of Process Management
- APQC (American Productivity and Quality Center: Process Classification Framework)
- Scheer Y–model

2. *Domain-specific reference models* from industry organizations
   - APQC (American Productivity and Quality Center: Process Classification Framework)
   - SCOR (Supply Chain Operations Reference Model from the Supply Chain Council)
   - DCOR (Design Chain Operations Reference Model from the Supply Chain Council)
   - CCOR (Customer Chain Operations Reference Model from the Supply Chain Council)
   - VRM (Value Reference Model from the Value Chain Group)
   - ITIL (The IT Infrastructure Library)
   - Accenture Service Line Business Process Reference Models.
     - o HR
     - o Value-driven BPM (PoPM)
     - o SCM (supply chain management)
     - o CRM (customer relationship management)

3. *Software and IT reference models*
   - Software reference model as part of the software product (e.g., delivered by SAP or Oracle)
   - Software reference model positioned separately (e.g., by consulting companies)

4. *Procedural reference models* showing the best practices of specific procedures that are not part of the daily operational business of an organization (e.g., a project management reference model or a reference model to build business process governance)
   - Project Management (PMBOK)

5. *Company reference models* representing a best practice within a company or a company group (such as a sales process rolled out to all sales subsidiaries)
   * Siemens Reference Process House (RPH)
   * Air Products
   * Many others

Functional Model from Industry Organization: Supply Chain Operations Reference Model

Used worldwide, the Supply Chain Operations Reference Model (SCOR) from the Supply Chain Council has been around for more than a decade and is now in its tenth version.[5] It is a business-process reference model that contains all the supply chain activities, from a supplier's supplier to a customer's customer, including

* All customer interactions, from order entry through paid invoice
* All product (physical goods, services, etc.) transactions, including equipment, supplies, spare parts, bulk product, and software
* All market interactions, from the understanding of the aggregate demand to the fulfillment of each order

SCOR contains four levels of process detail, as shown in Figure 8-2. The top level (*process types*) defines the scope and content. It consists of the five top-level processes:

* Plan
* Source
* Make
* Deliver
* Return

The second level of SCOR, the configuration level, contains more than 30 *process categories*, such as make to stock, make to order, engineer to order, and production execution. These process categories can be used to configure a company's supply chain. Companies implement their operations strategy through the configuration they choose for their supply chain.

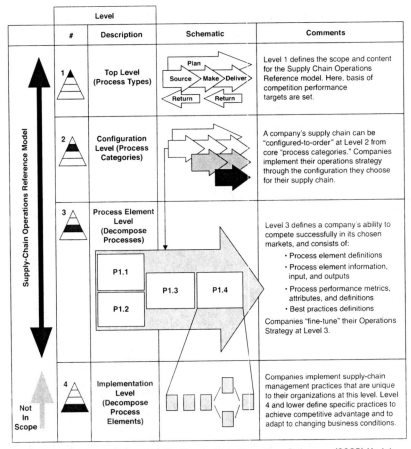

FIGURE 8-2. Levels Covered by the Supply Chain Operations Reference (SCOR) Model

P1.1: Identify, prioritize, and aggregate supply-chain requirements. P1.2: Identify, assess, and aggregate supply-chain requirements. P1.3: Balance supply-chain resources with supply-chain requirements. P1.4: Establish and communicate supply-chain plans. Reprinted by permission of the Supply Chain Council

The third SCOR level, the *process element* level (*decompose processes*), fine-tunes the operations of a company. It consists of the following:

- Process element definitions
- Process element information, inputs, and outputs
- Process performance metrics
- Best practices
- System capabilities necessary to support best practices
- Systems and tools to be used

Value Chain
The horizontal chain with interdependent processes that generates benefits and value to the end user.

Strategic Processes
VRM coverage begins with Govern, Plan and Execute processes with aligned metrics that can be applied in a ValueCard to gain competitive advantage.

Tactical Processes
The second level of the model contains processes decomposed from the Strategy Level, supporting the implementation of strategic goals through tactical decisions and configurations.

Operational Processes
The third level of the model represents decomposed Tactical Level processes, establishing links between enterprise specific activities in the value chain.

Activities
A decomposition of VRM operational processes. Each activity is specific to an enterprise that may or may not be shared among partners.

Actions
Individual work instruction items. Cannot be decomposed.

FIGURE 8-3. Value Reference Model

Companies implement their supply chain solution on level four (or even more detailed levels). Level four, or the implementation level (*decompose process elements*), defines practices to achieve competitive advantage and to adapt to changing business conditions. This level is company-specific and not in the scope of SCOR.

Functional Model from an Industry Organization: Value Reference Model

The Value Reference Model (VRM) from the Value Chain Group focuses on the complete value chain.[6] It is a cross-industry, analytical model that establishes a classification scheme for business processes using a hierarchy of levels and relationships through inputs and outputs into a process. It establishes a contextual relationship with best practices and metrics to help classify the processes that are most critical to an enterprise.

Industry and Functional Model: APQC Process Frameworks

The American Productivity and Quality Center (APQC) is another industry organization that has been developing industry-centric and functional models since 1992, the best known of which are its Process Classification Frameworks (PCFs). Originally conceived to aid in performance management initiatives, the PCFs have since been expanded into broad BPM reference models. APQC has worked with Accenture, the Supply Chain Council, the Telecommunications Management Forum, and the Value Chain Group to help these organizations promote their own models. Industry and functional frameworks include the following categories:

- Aerospace and defense
- Automotive
- Banking
- Broadcasting
- Consumer products
- Education
- Electric utilities
- Petroleum downstream (refining, distribution)
- Petroleum upstream (extraction)
- Pharmaceutical
- Telecommunications

Software-Based Reference Models

Vendors of ERP systems, in part to clarify the business content of their systems, have made great strides in developing reference models that link the software applications with usable business content.

As one of the major vendors of ERP software, SAP has invested a great deal of its experience with enterprise processes into reference models. The processes enabled by its ERP software now comprise one of the major reference models on the market. Oracle and the standards organization OASIS also offer reference models.

Industry Reference Model from Academia: Scheer Y-Model

Scheer's Y-Model is a reference model for industrial enterprises that has been adapted to multiple industry sectors. The top level of the Y-Model for discrete manufacturing companies is shown in Figure 8-4. The left side of the Y displays all order-related processes, and the right side shows all product-focused processes. Horizontally, the Y

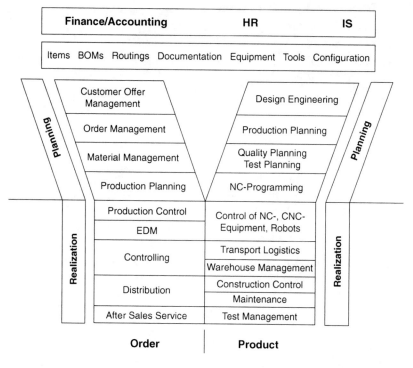

FIGURE 8-4. Scheer Y-Model

(After A.-W. Sheer)

captures the processes in execution and planning. The core support processes are defined above the Y.

Most people, even BPM practitioners, are not aware of the breadth and scope of work that goes into creating reference models. Once people become aware, two things usually happen: they seek reference models that can be applied to their business directly or that can act as inspiration, and they start considering creating their own reference models for specific parts of their business as a form of knowledge capture. The information just presented can help with either of these activities.

Notes

1. August-Wilhelm Scheer, *ARIS: Business Process Frameworks*, 3rd ed. (Berlin: Springer-Verlag, 2000);

Carol O'Rourke, Neal Fishman, and Warren Selkow, *Enterprise Architecture Using the Zachman Framework* (Boston: Course Technology, 2003);

Anne Lapkin, "The Seven Fatal Mistakes of Enterprise Architecture," Gartner Research publication, ID-number: G00126144, February 22, 2005; and

James McGovern, Scott W. Ambler, Michael E. Stevens, James Linn, Vikas Sharan, and Elias K. Jo, *A Practical Guide to Enterprise Architecture* (Upper Saddle River, NJ: Prentice-Hall, 2004).

2. August-Wilhelm Scheer, *Business Process Engineering: Reference Models of Industrial Enterprises,* 2nd ed. (Berlin: Springer-Verlag, 1994);

Peter Fettke and Peter Loos, eds, "Classification of Reference Models: A Methodology and Its Application," *Information Systems and E-Business Management*, 1(1): 35–53; and

Wolfram Jost, *EDV-gestuetzte CIM Rahmenplanung.* (Wiesbaden: Gabler, 1993).

3. August-Wilhelm Scheer, *Business Process Engineering: Reference Models for Industrial Enterprises,* 2nd ed. (Berlin: Springer-Verlag, 1994);

Peter Fettke and Peter Loos, "Classification of Reference Models: A Methodology and Its Application," *Information Systems and E-Business Management*, 1(1): 35–53;

Wolfram Jost, *EDV-gestuetzte CIM Rahmenplanung* (Wiesbaden: Gabler, 1993);

Peter Fettke and Peter Loos, eds, *Reference Modeling for Business Systems Analysis* (Hershey, PA: Idea Group, 2007), 1–20; and

Mathias Kirchmer, *Business Process Oriented Implementation of Standard Software: How to Achieve Competitive Advantage Efficiently and Effectively,* 2nd ed. (Berlin: Springer-Verlag, 1999).

4. American Productivity and Quality Center, "Using Process Frameworks and Reference Models to Get Real Work Done: APQC Best Practices Report," APQC 2011.

5. Supply Chain Council, ed., "Supply Chain Operations Reference Model: Plan, Source, Make, Deliver, Return," Version 8.0, 2007.

6. Value Chain Group, ed., "Value Reference Model: VRM Methodology Coverage," accessed July 31, 2011, http://www.value-chain.org/value-reference-model/.

PART III

The Present and the Future of Value-Driven BPM

CHAPTER 9

Value-Driven BPM in Practice

Companies across a range of industries have successfully put value-driven BPM into practice. Each one faced unique challenges and choices when using BPM to address the issues, but all shared the experience of extremely rewarding BPM implementations.

In this chapter, we take a closer look at four examples. From oil and gas, and high-tech engineering, to chemicals and services, each of these companies recognized that a Process of Process Management (PoPM) for value-driven BPM was needed to help optimize processes, eliminate duplicative software and wasteful practices, and boost efficiency. These real-life experiences—derived from an engagement with some of the largest and most influential companies in their industries—also illustrate how value-driven BPM comes to life in a series of steps toward increasing maturity.

In every case, the critical element that resolves classical conflicts between business objectives is transparency, as highlighted in the value pairs discussion in Chapter 2. This is one of the primary outcomes of implementing a PoPM in each case.

CASE STUDY 1: VALUE-DRIVEN BPM AT A GLOBAL OIL AND GAS COMPANY

A global oil and gas company used value-driven BPM to support postmerger integration. After the merger, the company was left with a raft of redundant business processes, creating an impediment to compliance with ever-stricter regulations. The case for alignment was compelling: At one of our first visits, a senior executive told us, "It

Company Characteristics	Large oil and gas company with 30,000 employees
Triggers	Merger and acquisition rationalization
Value Pairs	Compliance — agility transparency
Process Reference Model for PoPM	

BPM Operations

BPM Maturity and Value Analysis	Process Value Analysis	Roadmap	Governance

BPM Methods and Tools

Business Architecture			
Standards and Guidelines	Process Improvement Methods		
Repository	BPM Systems		

BPM Delivery

Process Strategy	Process Analysis
Process Design	Process Implementation
Process Execution	Process Monitoring

BPM Transformation

Culture and People Change Management
BPM Community
Program and Project Management

BPM Support

Finance	Procurement	HR	Enterprise Services	IT

FIGURE 9-1.

doesn't really help us to save money here or there. If we don't meet our safety and compliance requirements, that will kill us. That's what we have to focus on." Through creating a BPM Center of Excellence (CoE), selecting a repository tool, and creating a strategic roadmap, the company now has a harmonized and unified business process, reducing risk and improving transparency. (See Figure 9-1.)

Trigger: Merger and Acquisition Rationalization

The oil and gas company merged with another company in its market and found itself with a morass of business processes from both companies, some of which were duplicative or met varying, redundant process standards. Not only were these processes designed to different standards but they also were characterized by several BPM tools and environments. Visibility into tasks and workflows was very limited, and in a highly regulated industry, it is imperative to comply with processes and procedures dictated by international safety, health, and environmental laws. With a surplus of standards and repositories in hand, there was a clear need to improve BPM capabilities. The company was experiencing tension in the compliance-agility value pair and needed to achieve postmerger integration and develop a mechanism to enforce compliance. Aware of the improvements to efficiency and transparency that would result from a comprehensive transformation of BPM capabilities, the company set out to establish a flexible, streamlined platform to support new and improved BPM capabilities and to build a single repository for all business processes, process models, and related content. To do this, the company needed to replace multiple BPM tools with one best-of-breed platform. Our engagement helped the company narrow the field of potential vendors and platforms.

How Value-Driven BPM Helped

Value-driven BPM helped the company make progress in numerous areas, touching many of the process areas in the Process of Process Management.

We held a workshop on repositories (BPM Methods and Tools: Standards and Guidelines/Repository), which defined new, standard processes to use throughout the organization. To create a workable approach for running the repository, we established standards and guidelines for the modeling. Starting with a reference model accelerated the effort; without those guidelines, there would be no rubric for storing the models that would make them easy to retrieve.

We conducted a Process Value Analysis (BPM Operations) to analyze the process capabilities, beginning with those that were already well established. As safety is a prime concern of any energy company involved in extracting resources, the first area of focus was on content around existing safety and compliance procedures. Those procedures were added to the process models. Then, to better distribute the content, the company added a workflow system to route forms and documents related to governance and safety through the organization.

One of the most important tasks was to select a BPM platform that would support all of the process models for the company, including a new workflow system (BPM Methods and Tools). We helped the company define requirements, solicit and review proposals, and settle on a short list of software vendors. The company ultimately selected ARIS.

Seeking a more standardized, best-practice approach to BPM, the company created a global BPM Center of Excellence (CoE) that would own the PoPM going forward (BPM Operations: Governance). On the human side, the CoE optimizes internal standards for process management, develops roles, and sets requirements for CoE staff as well as process owners in numerous departments. On the software side, the CoE provides modeling services, conducts modeling workshops, and delivers tool support and BPM model conversions.

The BPM CoE has generated cost savings and efficiency for the company by right-sizing the BPM staff and establishing a single point of contact for process improvement proposals and other BPM initiatives. The CoE houses knowledge about how to leverage BPM in the future. The next task for the CoE is to provide process-monitoring control and enterprise architecture modeling, which includes applications, data, and other technical components.

In addition to addressing near-term BPM challenges, the oil and gas company also needed an end-to-end, value-driven BPM strategy. To achieve this, we conducted sessions with the company's BPM leadership, as well as group workshops with process owners and stakeholders, to develop a clear understanding of the company's BPM objectives, capabilities, and challenges (BPM Operations). We conducted a maturity assessment and a process value analysis of the company's BPM capabilities and the relative value of its processes. The result of this work was a comprehensive, holistic BPM strategy that included roadmaps to the company's future BPM needs as well as governance and operation of its process models. The roadmap also defined BPM roles outside of the CoE, such as process owners.

The company is now in the process of identifying its most critical IT capabilities (BPM Support) to support the BPM enterprise architecture, which contains the process models and applications that directly support the company's processes.

To implement the changes that came from the new workflow, the standardized process models, and the selection of new BPM software, the BPM Delivery subprocess, particularly Process Design and Process Execution, was put into motion (BPM Delivery).

Ultimately, most of the Process of Process Management was used to deliver a new level of capability at the oil and gas company. BPM methods and tools added process around BPM systems and managing the workflow component. BPM operations helped establish governance through a Center of Excellence and a roadmap. The roadmap determined the changes needed in systems (BPM Methods and Tools), for which a delivery mechanism was needed (Process Design and Process Execution). In the future, the company will work to further incorporate value-driven BPM into its overall culture (BPM Transformation).

Measurable Results

Success in the oil and gas industry depends on compliance with health, security, and environmental regulations. This company now has a harmonized and unified business process that improves transparency and reduces tension in the compliance-agility value pair, reduces risk of violating regulations, and reduces the time and effort required for ensuring process compliance with both internal and external standards. The company achieved a globally standardized approach to BPM and a uniform level of process quality. Through its CoE, there is now a schema for baking value-driven BPM into the corporate DNA.

The bottom-line impacts of these changes include reduced operating costs, improved efficiency through automation of key business processes, and the replacement of four BPM tools with one best-of-breed solution. The transparency gained from implementing value-driven BPM also affords better visibility into cost-saving opportunities in other areas beyond safety and compliance.

> We were particularly impressed by the ability of two very proud organizations to rally around a central framework. We helped the company create a common skeletal framework that the COO was able to use as a rallying point. All parties were quick to contextualize their most valuable nuggets into a common structure. The COO stated that the reference framework was a great catalyst for change.

CASE STUDY 2: MAJOR HIGH-TECH ENGINEERING COMPANY

A high-tech engineering company needed to vastly increase its manufacturing and engineering capacity for a government contract while meeting the government's budget requirements and maintaining sufficient margins. Through process simulation, the company was able to design and simulate engineering processes and relate those processes to IT and business objectives. It also scuttled a plan to add staff, which would have raised costs and relocated, rather than removed, a bottleneck. Evidence-based surveying techniques revealed further inefficiencies and misalignments. In addition to meeting production and quality requirements, correcting these issues using value-driven BPM meant that the company could now effectively model processes, clear bottlenecks, correctly assign resources, and maintain a sustainable, well-governed BPM capability. (See Figure 9-2.)

Trigger: Innovation and Growth

The excitement that comes with a major new contract can be followed by trepidation. How best to expand capacity in a way that meets budget yet maintains sufficient margins and levels of quality? This company had to use performance-based logistics to guarantee an agreed-on level of performance and systems capability, which would also require the company to deliver a certain number of products each year in a multiyear contract. How could the leadership be sure that existing processes could produce 10 times as many products in five years? That burning question drove the main goals of the value-driven BPM project:

- Increase the scalability and flexibility of the engineering and manufacturing process.
- Identify and eliminate the root causes of inefficiency, delays, and defects.

The general manager of the business unit told us, "I am pretty sure we have to invest and adjust our processes to the growing demand. But I don't have the transparency to know exactly what to do."

The initial thought was to use the company's existing BPM modeling and repository tool, the ARIS Toolset, to model engineering processes. While an important part of the strategy, this alone would not provide all of the insights needed to optimize process flow. The company also needed new process simulation skills in order to test process flows and configurations of work before implementing the solutions, as well as the necessary governance to keep those solutions highly functional.

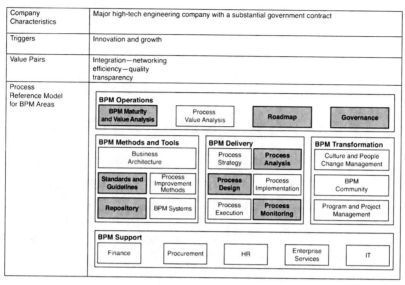

Company Characteristics	Major high-tech engineering company with a substantial government contract
Triggers	Innovation and growth
Value Pairs	Integration—networking efficiency—quality transparency

FIGURE 9-2.

How Value-Driven BPM Helped

The consulting engagement began with an analysis through interviews in one business unit. The objective was to achieve transparency, the center of the value-pair diagram (see Figure 2-1). Once the interview program was completed, the company had a healthy head start toward value-driven BPM.

Next, the company began building a repository to store process models (BPM Methods and Tools: Repository).

Once the repository was well developed, the next step was to simulate existing processes and begin to make changes to those processes (BPM Delivery: Process Analysis). That meant adding qualitative data to the repository in order to begin the simulations. Bottlenecks began to reveal themselves, unmasking opportunities to improve throughput, scalability, and functional integration. Quickly, the company could see where small investments would begin to reap immediate results. Once results began to show up in one business unit, the company gained the confidence to begin simulations in other business units and roll out the successful approach.

Before spreading the simulation efforts, the company needed to create a CoE (BPM Operations: Governance) so that the repository could be leveraged centrally. The CoE helped create a roadmap

(BPM Operations: Roadmap) so that the company could define an outcome-driven BPM strategy.

The simulation had numerous results. It illustrated alignment between the organization at large and the engineering process, as well as how changes to staffing would affect performance. Signs of future trouble came to light: manufacturing planning staff were often overwhelmed and unable to keep up with the increased workload, which then caused major delays in the downstream engineering process. The planning leaders believed they could increase planning productivity by 132 percent by boosting planning function staffing by 59 percent.

The proposal appeared to have a solid business case, but the process simulation revealed that the planning function's increased productivity would have no impact on engineering. Instead, there would be a new bottleneck between planning and engineering. It also revealed similarly critical integration points between engineering and several departments:

- Scheduling
- Procurement
- Manufacturing
- Tooling
- Production control
- Planning
- Quality
- Configuration management

Further benefits of the process simulation included raised awareness about how changes to a single aspect of the engineering process would affect overall process performance. This allowed the company to put optimized processes in place and ensure that the optimized processes would support long-term success.

The simulation exercise had a tremendous follow-on effect in the rest of the organization, spurring additional projects that included two key initiatives:

- *Applying process design to all of the key engineering processes:* Simulations of engineering processes could determine the precise combination of structure and supporting resources that would result in optimal performance.

- *Developing an overall BPM strategy:* The high-tech company had many overlapping and redundant BPM projects. Many of the processes were inefficient because the projects overlapped, wasting effort. The solution was to conduct a survey-based BPM Maturity Assessment (BPM Operations: BPM Maturity and Value Analysis). The assessment consisted of interviews with company functional heads and executive leadership about their BPM objectives and their pain points—reconciling the two and fine-tuning BPM objectives that were off the mark relative to the problems they were trying to solve. At this time, the consulting team also analyzed cross-functional tools and capabilities, ultimately developing an overall BPM strategy that clearly outlined the company's BPM goals, limitations, and capabilities.

Measurable Results

Ultimately, the value-driven BPM process simulation capability at the high-tech engineering firm enabled the company to:

- Gain transparency into engineering processes
- Test scenarios of production volume
- Locate and clear bottlenecks in a critical business unit, which paved the way for wider use of BPM
- Confidently identify areas for improvement and the resources needed at each stage of the improvement program
- Scale at the pace required by the contract
- Reduce redundancy
- Focus investments in capacity, with minimal waste
- Experience smooth integration with more than 2,000 suppliers and partners
- Keep a $120 million system implementation on track by revealing integration points between the new system and functional areas

One of the core points of value-driven BPM is that the skills developed during a specific exercise can then be recycled into a management discipline that continuously improves process management at an organization. This was the case at the high-tech engineering firm, which now has a durable BPM capability based on repository management, a governance structure that includes a CoE and new standards and guidelines, and better visibility into the interrelationships among its people, functions, and processes—critical to its ability to formulate effective strategies and achieve lasting value.

CASE STUDY 3: GLOBAL CHEMICAL COMPANY

A global chemical company provides chemical, plastic, and agricultural products and services to customers in 175 countries. Grappling with postmerger integration, the company was challenged with rolling out its SAP ERP platform and deriving as much value from it as possible. After establishing an effective methodology for aligning business processes to the new capabilities in the ERP platform, the company discovered that its core business processes are now more scalable, efficient, and agile, it gets better returns on SAP through BPM, and it is able to offer better customer and competitive value. (See Figure 9-3.)

Triggers: Core Systems Implementation and M&A

As part of its ongoing evolution as a leading global business and its pursuit of high performance, the company had embarked on the implementation of a new SAP ERP platform to integrate the acquisition of a new company. This large-scale implementation was intended to support myriad key functions, including finance, supply chain management, human resources, procurement, and plant maintenance. While the potential benefits of the planned SAP implementation were significant—including increased integration, efficiency, and agility—the project also required rapid and substantial improvements to a host of business processes that supported the affected functions. Further, the company needed to standardize processes after its merger.

How Value-Driven BPM Helped

The overall objectives of the project were to integrate an acquired company, improve core business processes, derive as much business value as possible from the new SAP system, and improve the usability and transparency of those processes through a business process

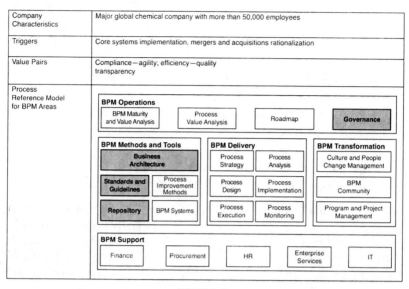

Company Characteristics	Major global chemical company with more than 50,000 employees
Triggers	Core systems implementation, mergers and acquisitions rationalization
Value Pairs	Compliance—agility; efficiency—quality transparency
Process Reference Model for BPM Areas	

FIGURE 9-3.

repository. Value-driven BPM was used for a process-oriented SAP implementation, with a focus on business outcomes that went beyond technology.

The first task was to establish an effective methodology for redesigning processes, while integrating the new platform at the same time. The consulting team planned an end-to-end project that included the documentation of existing processes (BPM Delivery: Process Analysis), the identification of process requirements to support the new SAP-enabled business process, and the identification of the capabilities needed to ensure reusability of design artifacts (BPM Methods and Tools: Repository, Standards and Guidelines, Business Architecture).

Once the project plan and methodology were defined, the team collaborated to align the full spectrum of the company's business processes with industry-specific best practices, the company's overall goals, and its new SAP platform. To do so, the team worked with the company's work stream and its functional teams to model and harmonize the company's business processes.

The team was able to use close integration of those process models with Accenture's preconfigured system and predeveloped ERP assets, including configuration scripts, technical process models, industry-specific application components, and project documentation.

At this company, the Accenture team worked closely with the company's management and process owners to build a state-of-the-art process repository using the ARIS platform (BPM Methods and Tools: Repository, BPM Systems). This repository, which integrates seamlessly with the company's SAP Solution Manager, is designed to help it house and manage its optimized business processes into the future. Throughout the engagement, the process repository was filled with working models of each new or improved process.

To keep the repository useful, the staff needed training and coaching. The consulting team was able to help the company design and deliver training on multiple aspects of BPM, including basic skills, blueprinting, and quality assurance. To ensure the sustainability of process improvements and value-driven BPM, the company established a CoE and an internal Community of Practice (CoP) (BPM Operations: Governance). This dedicated CoP is a permanent group within the company, focused on resolving issues with modeling methodology and ARIS product functionality, managing updates to modeling standards, and ensuring that the company benefits from the full functionality of the ARIS platform.

Measurable Results

This project has had a substantial positive impact. The company has transformed its core business processes to be more scalable, efficient, and agile. This transformation means that not only will this chemicals company be able to reap more substantial returns on its SAP investments, but it will also enjoy both immediate and long-term customer and competitive value that will help support its ongoing pursuit of high performance.

CASE STUDY 4: GLOBAL SERVICES COMPANY

A major global services company set out to optimize the applications that best supported the processes for each of its businesses and to improve the links between applications and processes. It wanted to drive efficiency by cutting IT costs through standardizing and rationalizing redundant applications, and by improving the quality and consistency of its customer service at the same time. With Accenture's help, the company set about implementing value-driven

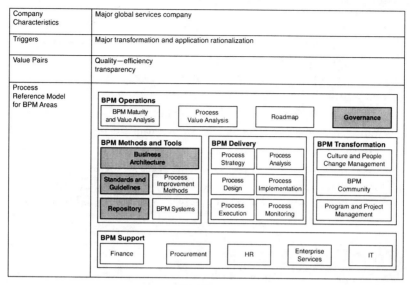

FIGURE 9-4.

BPM. By using an industry-specific BPM process model, documenting its existing operational model and processes through three layers of hierarchy (see Chapter 4), and assigning specific applications to specific processes, IT could now understand how processes were affected by different approaches to application design, coding, testing, and deployment, and could also better align technology investments with business objectives. This also produced greater operational transparency, efficiency, and agility. (See Figure 9-4.)

Trigger: Major Transformation and Application Rationalization

A recent Accenture study found that high-performance businesses in the client's industry tend to have mastery of standardized processes and an IT department that is well integrated with those processes, which has enabled such businesses to deliver results to shareholders that are up to 50 percent higher than those of their peers over a three-year period.

The global services company was focused on identifying applications that best support processes for each of its businesses. Part of the trouble was that each major division had operated something like a fiefdom and was not integrated well with the others; having grown through mergers and acquisitions, the company was also widely geographically distributed. Additionally, through these acquisitions, the company had numerous redundant systems. The redundancy was dragging down performance of the company as a whole, particularly as IT had to support custom development in each division. The cost of managing IT was spinning out of control, with little money or resource capacity left for new development.

Standardizing and rationalizing applications became a priority. To meet this objective, the company had to understand exactly how each application impacted a key business process and then prioritize its IT rationalization plan accordingly. Otherwise, essential applications could be eliminated and low-value applications retained by mistake.

How Value-Driven BPM Helped

The project had the following objectives:

- Improving understanding of connections between applications and business processes
- Prioritizing the IT rationalization project accordingly
- Ensuring alignment of critical processes with strategy and industry best practices
- Providing the necessary tools, infrastructure, techniques, and coaching for future process management

> When we discussed the project objectives with the CIO, he said, "We have developed an inventory of our 2,500 applications. It's a masterpiece—but we have no way of deciding what to switch off! Give us an answer to this!" That was essentially our project brief.

The first step was to document the operating model and create an overarching view of the company's major process areas (BPM Methods and Tools: Business Architecture). The quickest and most efficient way to do this was to use an industry-specific BPM reference model that incorporated important lessons from hundreds of projects conducted in the sector. The industry-specific process model was critical to accelerating the modeling and improvement of the company's core processes so that the company could begin realizing value from the initiative more quickly.

The reference model was built into the Oracle BPA Suite, an OEM version of the supporting ARIS Toolset (BPM Methods and Tools: Business Architecture, Repository). A process map of the entire organization was created quickly. From this overview, the organization selected eight pilot process areas for improvement.

It was also key to this engagement that the PoPM be built and fortified so that future process challenges could be met head-on, garnering competitive advantage. To fulfill this goal, we worked with the client to develop and master a customized methodology to define and document the organization's business processes at a detailed level. Doing so enabled the company to more effectively refine and adapt its processes as business conditions and requirements changed. We also trained 15 of the company's business and IT employees on the best ways to conduct workshops with subject-matter experts and document processes in the repository, ultimately creating a BPM practice and CoE at the company (BPM Operations: Governance). Much of this training was hands-on. For instance, Accenture and company employees executed two work streams focused on the company's rating and pricing processes, capturing key activities, organizational roles, improvement opportunities, and system and application linkages across divisions.

As IT and applications were so essential to the functioning of the company, it was also important to adopt a process perspective for the application development life cycle. With this new perspective in place, IT could not only understand how its processes were affected by existing approaches to application design, coding, testing, and deployment, but also better align its technology investments with the company's overall business objectives.

Measurable Results

As a result of this project, the global services company deepened its understanding of the connections between its applications and its core business processes, laying the groundwork for a better approach to application rationalization and providing significant cost savings. The company now has the ability, tools, and associated application systems it needs to define and manage its business processes more effectively. The use of industry process reference models from Accenture accelerated time to transformation, as the competitive services industry's best practices were already embedded in the reference models. Prior to this engagement, the company's division presidents could not agree on an overall operating model of the company, having tried to do so organically for more than a year. Using a BPM reference model, the organizational model was created in six weeks. This resulted in greater operational efficiency and quality that ultimately enhanced the company's ability to achieve high performance. Furthermore, by defining, documenting, and centrally storing processes utilizing the ARIS repository, the client organization is now better equipped to maintain or improve existing processes and design new processes.

The client is also able to reduce operating costs by integrating and aligning work between the IT and business teams, by more effectively implementing future corporate initiatives, and by standardizing processes across business units, thus reducing redundant work and boosting efficiency. The company continues to standardize its application environment—an effort that will be aided significantly by the long-lasting, value-driven BPM capability now in place.

CHAPTER 10

The Future of Value-Driven BPM

Will value-driven BPM change the world? At this point, we hope you join us in answering this question with an enthusiastic "yes." In these pages, we have looked at how value-driven BPM works and why it matters to businesses, public sector organizations, and any large group of people that attempts to get work done effectively. Now it is time to take a step back and examine what the future holds for value-driven BPM. What are the forces that will drive more and more companies toward adoption? What struggles and transformations will occur during the journey? How will value-driven BPM change the way we think about business?

If you look at accelerating rates of change in the business world, the vastly increased complexity of organizations of all sizes, the previously unachievable distribution of responsibilities in value chains containing at times thousands of companies working together, it is clear that a new way of managing is being formed. The world is becoming more dynamic and technology is shrinking time and space, enabling communication and business relationships that would have been impossible a generation, let alone a century, ago. As *New York Times* columnist Thomas Friedman has pointed out, the world is indeed becoming flatter.[1]

This dynamic has created a tension in organizations. In the networked world, organizations are becoming less hierarchical, more social, and more global. Leaders recognize that the technology that is embodied in mobility, social media, crowdsourcing, smart devices, and myriad other forms is changing everything. This change needs to be embraced, but we also recognize that most organizations do not, will not—and probably should not—function like an emergent crowd on Facebook or Wikipedia. The answer is not simply to adopt more technology, open offices in 20 countries, and hope that everything will work.

To be sure, organizations need agility—the ability to respond to more stimuli and to act with greater precision. But agility does not mean that each response is invented anew. Agility is a combination of fast reactions and methodological, orderly thinking. The boundary between the millennials' trigger-happy stimuli response and the methodical ways of older generations is a fault line. As these two cultural tectonic plates grind together, new kinds of processes will emerge. Tracking these developments is central to our research and should be of interest to all BPM practitioners.

The greatest aid to agility, or any of the other core values of an organization, is transparency, which switches the lights on so that we can balance the design of each process, allowing freedom to innovate here, restricting choices there, and asking for approvals in other cases. Intelligent use of BPM ensures that we aren't too rigid—stifling the network effect and revolutionary triumphs of Enterprise 2.0, 3.0, and beyond, while also providing a guide for moving forward in an orderly fashion—so that organizations don't drown in a sea of ideas or collectively tread water in a tide pool.

Agility is not just about moving fast and changing fast. It's also about discovering fast, capturing knowledge fast, and propagating knowledge and practices fast. The right shape for each organization may be discovered through experimentation, and then should be captured in process descriptions. Process is the abstraction that can manage the chaos of the new world—technology cannot do it alone. Value-driven BPM allows us to keep track of the shape while it is changing.

While a focus on process helps balance the degrees of freedom required to innovate and exhibit virtuosity with the need for standardization and order, it is the concept of value that provides the compass and helps us determine what matters in the maze of choices we all face. The agility demanded by the world we work in now requires that processes be directly connected to outcomes of value—there simply isn't time or overhead available to commit to process initiatives that don't make or save money for the organization or allow the company to tangibly improve results that customers will pay for.

In 2010, Accenture's global BPM practice participated in engagements with more than 70 top-tier clients, in which the primary focus was on adopting an outcome-based and value-driven approach to BPM. Through our discussions with CEOs, CIOs, CFOs, and COOs, we confirmed that process is one of the chief competitive assets an organization can have. Creating competitive advantage through individual products or services is not enough. Such advancements can be copied too quickly. We believe that the management of process is itself a C-level priority because it is the path to lasting competitive differentiation. Whether or not a company actually establishes a C-suite position such as chief process officer (CPO) depends a great deal on the personalities and management style of the current executives and the intensity of the need to improve processes at the organization. But it is clear that as process assets become more valuable, organizations need to take more responsibility for baking good process management practices into everything they do. That's what this book has been about.

TRENDS AND PREDICTIONS: HOW VALUE-DRIVEN BPM WILL SHAPE THE WORLD OF BUSINESS

There are two ways we want to help you chart your journey forward as this book comes to a conclusion. First, we examine trends that are leading companies to increase their commitment to value-driven BPM as a management practice and also address the problems that will occur as adoption increases. There are several common points of pain affecting virtually every industry that can be addressed effectively through value-driven BPM. By looking at these trends and at the challenges related to BPM adoption, it is possible to get ahead of the curve and act before a point of pain becomes a crisis. Second, we make predictions on how that transformation will take place. What are the milestones along the way? What decisions should companies prepare to make? How will organizations and roles be forced to change? These predictions are more subjective than the trends we've identified, but they are based on our experience and give some food for thought. The chapter concludes with a look at the way value-driven BPM will change what it means to manage a business.

TRENDS: WHAT'S DRIVING COMPANIES TOWARD VALUE-DRIVEN BPM

The following six trends support our argument that the complexity and speed of change in both business and technology will drive companies toward value-driven BPM.

Trend 1: A Real-Time, Heads-Up Business Environment

In Chapter 1 and throughout this book we have outlined the forces that are making the business world an arena of continuous transformation. Population growth, technology, energy, environmental concerns, heightened health and terrorism risks, roiling financial markets, and globalization are all conspiring to increase the pace of change, risk, and complexity. In the face of these challenges, businesses compete with each other to execute an accelerated response. The world is highly dynamic, and pressure is mounting to expand new business and optimize the supply chain while holding down costs.

Remember the business cycle? Remember the five-year planning horizon? Remember when companies with revenue measured in the billions were always decades old? Modern business has shed such quaint artifacts as the annual cycles of strategic retreats, budgeting, planning, execution, and monitoring. Today, all of these activities increasingly are taking place on a continuous basis.

The ability to react to change and continue to maintain and improve the connection between process and value will be one of the defining characteristics of high-performance businesses and public sector organizations.

What executives really need is a management system tailored to this reality. The closest we get to seeing such systems that would help manage the environment is movies like *Iron Man* and *Minority Report*. Information is analyzed based on highly interactive, malleable, visual displays. The characters in these movies have urgent problems to solve. They look to the data to figure out what to do.

What is never explored in these movies is how this all would actually work. If you are zooming in and out of mountains of data, how do you know what is important? How do you know what data-set out of thousands or millions matters? How are hundreds of technology systems orchestrated? What are the principles used to organize everything? How does it change? Value-driven BPM provides answers to all of these questions.

Trend 2: Meshing "Dynamic Change" and "Slow and Steady"

Future shock, the fear that the world is moving so fast we cannot keep up, and *information anxiety*, the fear that there is too much information and we cannot know what is important, are no longer novel conceptual ideas. They are a way of life. If we are going to create the heads-up displays we need to organize the information we look at and the actions we take; if we are going to turn business into a complex, ever-shifting video game—not with one world to explore but with dozens or even hundreds—we are going to have to construct a model of what we are doing that will bring everything into focus. Process is the foundation of this model. Process is the abstraction that organizes and conquers the complexity of this new world.

We now live in a time when the need for rapid stimuli response is being woven into the fabric of society, which naturally permeates organizations. This is the era of networks, social media, video games, and the interplay between many types of media—the province of the so-called millennial generation. Everyone wants, and is expected to deliver, just about everything, right about now, and the companies that can achieve speed, whether it's shoes delivered overnight or an instant car-loan approval, are increasingly the most successful.

By contrast, prior generations have always built success on a methodological approach. The boundary between agility and order is where process lives, and in some ways, the role of value-driven BPM is to forge an optimal compromise. That boundary needs to be well defined and protected. Imagine the boundary as viewed from above. It won't take the shape of a straight line. Instead, it may look like a serrated line of teeth, where innovation and process discipline push against each other until they interlock, forming a tight mesh of value. One could also think of this interaction as a "demilitarized zone" of compromise, where process excellence tames the manic energy of innovation, creating a smooth and reliable operation. This boundary cannot be so rigid as to stifle the innovation promised by Enterprise 2.0+, but it also cannot be so loose that mayhem envelops large enterprises and strategic direction becomes obscured in a sea of individual initiatives.

Process is also a calming and directing force for the change that is currently rifling through world markets, the supply chain, and product design and pricing. Products that were once designed in the West, manufactured in the East, and shipped back to the West now have a much more complex life cycle that may mean design, sales, production, and distribution happen in multiple geographies, and flows are multidirectional. (After all, if the fastest-growing market in the world is in Asia, shipping Asian manufactured goods back to the West may happen to a lesser extent, if at all.) To manage these flows, organizations need rock-solid processes, and value-driven BPM ensures that the planning and management of those processes is on solid footing.

Financial regulation is also driving the quest for more precision and process definition. In the United States, Sarbanes-Oxley Article 422 declares that companies must develop a scheme to document how they create value, if they have nonaccounting assets. Regulations such as this will increase pressure to improve transparency and documentation of how processes achieve value.

We believe that the pressures we have summarized here will lead to an increased process orientation. Value-driven process design, based on transparency, will allow rapid change without a descent into chaos.

Trend 3: Going "Glocal": Addressing the Challenges of Process Governance

As companies globalize, the "local versus global standards" debate rises in prominence. As technology, especially consumer-style technology, becomes more pervasive in the enterprise, end users gain power and influence over how processes are executed. Rigid top-down hierarchies stifle the energy and creativity of the individual to improve processes. The lack of policies or guidance can lead to security breaches and chaos. Either extreme is flawed. The question is, who should make process choices?

A traditional top-down view would make the CIO responsible for global technology standards, but as companies have penetrated new markets, local connectivity, fidelity, and adaptation suffered, making purely global control an ungainly proposition. Running everything from "the bottom up" has drawbacks as well, because redundant sets of standards will be developed, and there is a lack of consensus and cohesion around common issues that affect the entire organization—this debate rages both within IT and throughout the enterprise.

What should be common? What should be unique? What are the implications of these answers for process mapping, modeling, and management?

Making choices about how to go "glocal"—in other words, finding the right combination of local and global governance for processes—is a major part of the roadmap creation process described in Chapter 4, and it is a decision that is likely to rise to the C-level, because the critical nature of these choices is increasing.

Trend 4: The Coming Shortage of Value-Driven BPM Skills

One of the common problems faced by companies that adopt value-driven BPM is finding experienced people to implement the Process of Process Management (PoPM). While it is possible to find people with skills related to specific process design and management tools, doing so is no guarantee of success, as we have pointed out in many ways. A tools-focused approach to BPM is doomed to failure.

Until BPM in general and value-driven BPM in particular become more widespread, the only remedy to this challenge is to grow your own expertise. Such training programs are usually housed within a Center of Excellence (CoE) under the chief process officer, or whoever is leading the effort toward greater process maturity. The advantage of creating such a program is that it allows people with established expertise in your business to add to their skill sets. The combination of PoPM training and intimacy with existing business processes is a powerful foundation for progress. The only drawback is that training takes time and money. Growing a new generation of PoPM experts will not happen overnight.

Trend 5: BPM-Washing

Another sure sign of success in the BPM market will come when more and more companies adopt a process-oriented approach. We have seen the phenomenon of "green-washing" as companies claim sustainability benefits, and "cloud-washing" as companies get on the cloud-computing bandwagon. BPM has been around longer than these trends and has had ups and downs in the market. But as efforts to increase process maturity start to show results, it is likely that companies will attempt to position their products as BPM-related. In other words, "BPM-washing" will begin.

Although this will complicate the identification and selection of technology that is truly focused on mature and effective BPM practices, it will also be a validation that value-driven BPM has gone mainstream.

Trend 6: BPM and the Changing Role of Information Technology

The world of IT, like the world of business, is changing at an accelerated rate and becoming more granular and distributed. Because of technologies such as service-oriented architecture (SOA), software as a service (SaaS), and cloud computing, modern CIOs face a significant management challenge, as their end users are now making choices to adopt technology directly, without the guidance or participation of the IT department. In other words, the monopoly control the IT department held over technology is ending. In the face of this loss of control, how will the CIO exert influence over which technology is adopted? How will adoption of technology affect the way the processes are executed? How is the portfolio of technology continually aligned and realigned with the business? A process-oriented way to manage IT is key to ensuring that the maximum business value is created from the application of technology.

The Growing Maze of Technology

The first problem facing CIOs is that the world of technology is becoming much more complex and difficult to manage. "Consumerization" refers to the fact that end users are adopting and using devices and software-as-a-service solutions directly to solve business problems. Almost all of these devices and applications are accessible through wireless networks. Mobility has profound effects for how data can be accessed and collected, and where and when applications can be used. Processes are going to change dramatically because of these capabilities.

Cloud computing will continue to change the relationship of physical assets to applications and computing outcomes, which deeply affects the IT purchasing and management processes. In addition, advanced sensors and smart devices that have their own intelligence and processing power will open up a whole new frontier for automation and analysis, especially in combination with wireless networking. The result is that instead of having 100 components in a technology landscape, a CIO is likely to face 1,000 or more. Granted, each of these components will be easier to configure and control, but making them all work together is the key challenge. A business expert with good command over process and value-driven BPM know-how will be in a better position to meet these challenges.

Aligning Technology and Business Needs

In the face of a technology architecture that has many more moving parts controlled by both IT and end users, ensuring that every asset serves the business will become all the more vexing.

At the micro level, the new, more granular portfolio of configurable technology holds tremendous promise for changing how processes are designed and executed. Being able to access data, to collect data, to perform analysis, and to take action in the field through intelligent mobile devices will enable new ways of working. Being able to tailor a work environment to the needs of those who play a key role in executing processes offers the potential for better decisions, faster action, and more effective automation.

At the macro level, the challenge is to understand how technology supports business. Most CIOs approach this challenge through the framework of enterprise architecture. The applications and infrastructure are described in detail. This description is then mapped to the parts of the business that are supported. In an environment of rapid change, the challenge is to keep this mapping alive. Without it, it is hard to decide where to invest and which technology to retire. An enterprise architecture is an essential tool for gaining the transparency to manage change and set priorities.

Process as an Organizing Framework

In our opinion, as described in Chapter 1, the complexity of managing the technology portfolio, overseeing the redesign of processes to take advantage of technology, and keeping IT aligned with the business will lead CIOs to become process champions. As a result, a mature approach to the Process of Process Management as embodied in value-driven BPM will increasingly provide a way to manage the complexity just reviewed.

- As the portfolio of IT becomes more granular and distributed, process modeling is a natural tool for organizing the way technology is used and for evaluating the potential impact of a new technology. A process model helps show what role each technology plays in a complex process and provides a way to clearly define the boundaries between what people do and what technology will do.

- A process model can become the foundation for a clear understanding of the as-is state as new process designs are considered. A clearly stated model helps make sure that the new process is implemented as intended, possibly using new technology or new sources of data and analysis. Then, based on experience, the process can be improved. BPM can be an effective knowledge-capture tool that keeps everyone on the same page.
- The analysis and documentation tools of the PoPM can help complete an enterprise architecture and create a far richer model of how technology supports a business. Where needed, process modeling can be carried to a very detailed level.

The extension of the tools of value-driven BPM to manage the complexity of IT is made more effective because of advances in technology itself and in the maturity of thinking about process.

Our belief is that CIOs will increasingly use a process framework to organize the application landscape and derive lasting value from it because there are no alternatives that will provide as much help. With a process model that helps organize the application of technology, apply the technology to specific processes, and keep track of the big picture, it is now possible to understand how those heads-up displays on the big screen might actually work. The end users of such systems would in effect be navigating and interacting with process models that were used to bring together all of the information, automation, analysis tools, and application functionality needed to get a specific job done. While few of us will have the sexy displays we have seen in the movies anytime soon, a process-focused approach to IT management means that we all can have more and more of such content and functionality over time.

PREDICTIONS: WHERE ARE WE GOING NEXT WITH VALUE-DRIVEN BPM?

The core of our argument for the rise in importance of value-driven BPM is that the organizations that have the best understanding of the interrelationships between value objectives, means of production, people, information technology, and processes are the organizations that stand to profit the most. Value-driven BPM will be widely adopted because, as we are seeing in practice, it consistently leads to business success. But none of the organizations we have worked with has been able to wave a magic wand and suddenly increase its process maturity. Because the PoPM is something that can be used by every department, from the top to the bottom of the management hierarchy, it is also something that takes time to adopt. There are many paths to process management maturity.

The predictions that we highlight in this section come from our experience in the field helping companies improve their process maturity. We believe that companies should be able to find inspiration and guidance from each of the topics analyzed here, all of which point to ways that value-driven BPM will be put to good use.

Prediction 1: The Emergence of Strong Process Leadership

At most organizations, there is rarely a fight over who gets to lead the initial charge toward process maturity. To be frank, this is usually because excitement over using value-driven BPM grows only after the management practice has been shown to produce results. Once it is agreed that process is a significant asset that needs direct management from a high level, a challenging discussion ensues. Who is the right person to lead the expansion of process skills in an organization? How does this affect the organization of the C-suite? Each company needs to find its own answer to this question.

Most C-level positions, such as chief information officer and chief marketing officer, came about because a burning issue in the field needed maximum commitment from management. The CIO, for example, became a C-level position when information technology became such a substantial part of the expense base—and such a critical competitive weapon—for many corporations that it simply had to be managed by someone with the right knowledge in close communication with the rest of the C-suite.

Some of these positions have been ephemeral because their roles were not clearly defined. For example, at the turn of the millennium, organizations were infatuated with the so-called knowledge economy and quickly set about trying to become "knowledge-based organizations." Since "knowledge" was identified as a prime objective, having a chief knowledge officer (CKO) came into style. But it quickly became evident that few understood what the role of a CKO should be and how that role was connected to other roles in the organization. The position gradually faded away. But process has been a critical part of organizations since the Industrial Revolution. The need to manage complexity in a holistic way is now elevating process to a high level of priority, where we believe it is likely to stay. Therefore, process leadership will continue to be a C-level priority. One variation of this trend will be the emergence of the chief process officer, a role that we believe can be clearly defined in most organizations and that will be enduring.

The Rise of the CPO

The creation of the CPO role is an increasingly common result of the discussion described in the previous section about different ways to treat the rising preeminence of process as an asset and the need to foster innovation and curtail chaos across a widely distributed organization. Although every organization is of course different, the CPO role will prove to be especially effective in diverse organizations. Creating such a role centralizes knowledge capture and learning about what works to improve process maturity. Two main factors are contributing to the rise of a CPO role:

- *Dysfunction of the C-suite, with global change as a backdrop.* Our research has found that, at the highest level, many organizations—despite whatever may be said about being a "team" in the corporate literature—function less like a team than a group of powerful individuals with fiefdoms under their control. As organizations become more turbulent and distributed, that kind of arrangement may need to change. The ability to integrate resources effectively becomes more important. As organizations expand their reach across geographies and increase the number of business lines under their umbrellas, the challenge of integration becomes greater. That challenge extends all the way up to the boardroom. To succeed, the "team" will have to start acting more like a team in the truest sense.

  Such a team could benefit from an internal observer who keeps the targets in sight and the methodology for reaching those targets at the top of the discussion. In the past, that role has been played by individuals, ranging from the general counsel to the head of human resources to outside consultants. If process is indeed the path to strategic value, the champion of process should have a seat in the boardroom and should play a role in integrating process efforts beyond the boardroom as well. The title may not always be "chief process officer," but a champion of process will be an important executive position at many enterprises in the near future.

- *The crisis of the CIO role.* Because information technology and process are already deeply connected and will only become more intertwined, there is considerable weight behind the theory that the CIO role may gradually transform into an orchestrator of processes. In 2004 in an article in the German publication *Harvard Business Manager*, Wolfram Jost proposed that an increased orientation on process was required for the CIO role to be most effective.[2] It's already well documented that the CIO role is changing. IT is becoming consumerized. Enterprise systems are becoming more intuitive for business users, and employees have already begun to expect IT to support their iPads, BlackBerrys, and other personal technology devices in the same way that it supports their desktops and network. The increasing number of IT services that can be outsourced or purchased as managed services means the CIO spends less time directly managing hardware and software and more time setting broad strategy for orchestrating packages of services from third-party providers. If "process as an asset" is on the rise in the same way the rise of "IT as an asset" created the CIO role, then connecting the CIO's role to the design and implementation of processes will be an important part of a CIO's future. Depending on the organization, the CIO may effectively become the CPO, or a CPO role may develop independently. It's an open question as to whether these would be equals at some organizations or whether one might be the superior of the other.

    Other contenders for the role of top value-driven BPM leader include the chief operating officer or, in more industrial companies, the chief quality officer.

The Skills of the CPO

Regardless of how the question is resolved, the fact remains that someone at a relatively high level of the organization will need the skills necessary to lead the organization to higher levels of process maturity. This requires the ability to assemble a broad process-centric view of the organization and to create, manage, and improve process assets and related tools and systems. Most important, the leader needs to be able to deftly manage the interventions aimed at improving both process skills and the quality and efficiency of processes. In other words, the leader should be an expert in the Process of Process Management and a master triangulator. The CPO has to be the process owner. Many current C-level executives still lack these skills.

The CPO role, or the process capacity in another C-level role, will coalesce when an organization considers process to be a strategically important asset and when tangible value, monetary or otherwise, can be attached to process. Power accrues to those who are able to handle critical uncertainties. The CIO position materialized because hardware and software are mission-critical and expensive. Now, the tools and methods of BPM, captured in software, reflect a large investment of intellectual property and are consequently mission-critical and expensive. It is increasingly likely that organizations will see a reason to hear the voice of process in the boardroom.

The Jazzy Side of Organizational Dynamics

As mentioned in Chapter 6, inspiration for process-oriented organizations can come from a somewhat counterintuitive sector—the arts. Consider a jazz band. The music emerges from a dynamic interplay between the innovation of individual players and the framework of a certain piece of music that provides, in effect, the rules for the innovation. The framework is supplied by the bandleader, who has a vision for how the piece should be structured. The players each play their role in bringing that structure to life. Without the innovation, you get the same piece played over and over until it is boring and unpleasant. Without the framework, there is no music at all. Each time, the sounds are different, with no unity or identity. At its best, process maturity is reflected in the structure of a jazz band. Everyone knows what to do to make the music, but everyone is also on the lookout for ways to make the outcome more pleasing by adding his or her special talents. In a way, everyone can be a leader and a follower at different times, with innovation happening on a structured basis that meshes with the overall piece of music, or the organization's process strategy.[3]

Prediction 2: Emerging Market Multinationals as Adopters of Value-Driven BPM

We've spent a little time identifying individuals within enterprises who stand the best chance of becoming process leaders. But what kind of enterprises will be process leaders in their industries? Evidence suggests emerging market multinationals may be the most likely type of company to innovate new processes and make the most robust investment in value-driven BPM first. Just as the wireless networks in many emerging countries are superior to those in developed countries, the speed to adoption of BPM may follow the same pattern. With no legacy to fight against, taking the optimal path to process maturity may be easier. Of course, corporations in more established geographies may be able to use value-driven BPM to catch up to their upstart competitors.

Emerging market multinationals have "grown up global" in that they have come to prominence in this highly connected era. A company that is growing in the twenty-first century does not have the same preconceptions about direct ownership of assets and functional activities that may hamper more aggressive forms of growth in older companies. The leadership of relatively new and aggressive companies does not suffer from the "not invented here" syndrome. They understand that infrastructure can be procured externally and seek to outsource contextual activities to allow increased focus on the core value-creating processes. They are extremely competitive, often entering markets that used to be exclusively dominated by Western firms (take auto manufacturing in China, for instance). If the object is to create a good product at a low cost, process excellence is paramount and thus a high management priority. Also, to be a CIO or CPO in an emerging market multinational means direct control of IT is not as important as maintaining the core processes of the enterprise. These may be the companies most open to the role of the CPO and the promise of value-driven BPM.

Prediction 3: Process-Focused KPIs and Visual Performance Management

We can also expect closer integration of process with key performance indicators (KPIs) and better management capabilities. True enterprise-wide performance management is well on its way to becoming a reality. BPM will be characterized by enhanced performance-monitoring tools and improved visibility into processes and how well they are working, so that the connection between changes to process and value is clearer, more predictable, and easier to achieve. The instrumentation and measurement of financial performance is being extended to process metrics, which show what is happening in the beginning, middle, and end of a process. By understanding what happens earlier in a process, it is possible to identify and head off problems sooner.

User interfaces for understanding performance will improve and become more intuitive and easier to distribute throughout the value chain. While the heads-up displays of the movies may be a ways off, it is not unrealistic to think that within a few years' time, 3D visualizations and simulations analogous to role-playing video games will become a regular part of process design. Defense organizations already use such tools to design better equipment and improve the performance of personnel in the field. While incredibly complex, in the end, the design of a fighter jet or a commando operation is nothing more than the implementation of a process. Although the image of a 3D avatar of oneself perfecting an order-to-cash operation for a retailer may be less exciting than sending an avatar charging into battle, it may prove to be no less valuable for the organization.

Prediction 4: Social Networking and Virtualization

Social network analysis and process governance are becoming more closely related as we charge forward into the "Facebook world." In the early days of business process reengineering, when processes broke down, the workarounds people developed resulted in chaotic and wildly differing processes between organizational units. Part of the reason for this was that people trusted each other more than they trusted systems. When processes fail, and people are supportive of the enterprise, they discover ways in which to work around the problem—this is an important characteristic of flexibility.

Now, the level of acceptance of revolutionary social media such as Facebook, Twitter, and other platforms indicates that people are more willing to place trust in systems when those systems are customizable and reflect the social networks people inhabit. This has strong implications for process design and governance in the enterprise. In Enterprise 3.0, social networks will fuse with enterprise processes.

There will always be a need for value-driven BPM to bring order to a chaotic world. But surrounding the essential order that reflects the process thinking of the organization, there will be increasing degrees of freedom. In the near future, an "intelligent environment" will connect everything to process libraries, capturing innovations as they happen and providing a window for analysis and optimization.

For example, when someone devises a workaround to a preordained process, that workaround will be documented electronically and can become part of the ever-growing process library. Ultimately, it may be dismissed as a nonoptimal aberration, but it could also be embraced as an innovation or set aside for future improvement. It won't disappear under the radar. But this idea capture also won't happen unless there are rules that establish how it will happen.

In another example, process modelers will increasingly work in environments that are characterized less by 2D diagrams and more by virtual-reality, real-time, immersive experiences. Imagine that there is a change in natural, political, or financial conditions at some point during the life cycle of a product or part. An RFID sensor in a box can communicate exactly where it is at any point in time. What if process designers could assemble and alter process models based on real-time events and external triggers, and redesign aspects of a process around that box while it is on a 15-hour flight over the ocean, changing its destination or redesigning the process to squeeze a few more dollars or hours out of the process? What if enterprises could do this year-round, around the clock? The technology exists today—the process models are on their way.

The more intelligence that is built into the enterprise, the more direct, immediate, and fungible a link exists among people, process, and technology. Business process management will begin to be characterized less by reams of reports unfurled at quarterly board meetings, and more by minute real-time adjustments to process, like air traffic control. As much as air traffic control requires quick decisions and real-time technology, it is also bound by well-honed processes, such as flight plans, that have changed and improved over 100-plus years of flight. And of course, just like any system, it still needs to improve—many people complain that air traffic control is stuck with 1930s radar technology and should switch to satellites and GPS. Here again, the technology exists, but the connection to value has yet to be made convincingly, despite the critical importance of air transport to worldwide commerce, and processes have yet to be designed to make this a reality.

Prediction 5: Process-Centric Systems Integration

Just as a process focus can be used to manage the complexity of a technology portfolio under the purview of the CIO, so it can also be an organizing framework for systems integration. Process-centric systems integration is gradually becoming more commonplace for a variety of reasons. Process-design software is starting to integrate better with other business systems and facilitate dynamic repository management. Process modeling and process management tools are starting to be more tightly integrated with the execution and work-flow engines, that is, the applications and other systems that execute the automation.

The large applications in the business world—ERP, CRM, SCM, and so on—have gradually increased their process-centricity. Many of them are not configured directly using process models. The same is happening for smaller and niche solutions. Standards like BPEL (Business Process Execution Language) are not yet implemented consistently, but as time goes on, it is likely the implementation of this and other standards will converge. Such standardization will pave the way for integration between systems to be defined at the level of process models instead of using complex configuration and custom coding using computer languages.

When this all works properly, making technology fit a business need gets much simpler. One result of this sort of integration is that larger players in the market will have an advantage because they will be able to allow process models to control more and more of the technology landscape. Niche players will be forced to merge with these larger players or find a way to seamlessly fit into the integrated system.

Once we get to the point where a process model that is independent of an execution or workflow engine can be used to help implement best practices tailored to a specific need, it is likely that the market for reference models will expand. The role of the BPM Center of Excellence may increasingly involve managing and selecting those models. The skills needed to manage an IT suite and a value-driven BPM strategy may not be so far apart in the near future.

A NEW MANAGEMENT PHILOSOPHY

At the beginning of this book, we asserted that value-driven BPM was a new management discipline, a practice that could be extended to every part of an organization and help show the way to a better department, division, corporation, or extended value chain. At this point, we hope you agree that a focus on process maturity, using the principles of value-driven BPM and the Process of Process Management, can pay substantial dividends for your business.

Enterprise processes in the future will need more flexibility and autonomy, but they will fail if they do not have governance that reflects the new reality. The loose-network, annotated review model of Wikipedia and the social network model of Facebook are just the beginning, and the two will fuse with validated BPM techniques described earlier in this book to create something we have not yet seen. The conversations in the C-suite of the future will begin and end with a look at processes. Just as executives demand a financial view of operations as a way to understand what is important, so too will they demand a process view to be able to determine what actions to take. A mature process environment will need good governance more than ever, and the foundation for this governance lies in value-driven BPM. Proving the connection to value will be essential, as will responsive, agile systems and people who can orchestrate and manage the universe of choices that will unfold before them. These process champions will be as important to enterprises as process itself. Our sincere hope is that you—the readers of this book—will become those process champions and join us in our efforts to use process as a force to improve business results.

Notes

1. Thomas Friedman, *The World Is Flat: A Brief History of the 21st Century* (New York: Farrar, Strauss and Giroux, 2005).

2. Wolfram Jost, "Vom CIO zum CPO," *Harvard Business Manager*, September 2004, 88–89.

3. Mathias Kirchmer, *High-Performance Through Process Excellence,* 2nd ed. (Berlin: Springer-Verlag, 2011).

Abbreviations

ABE	activity-based emission control
APQC	American Productivity and Quality Center
ARIS	Architecture of Integrated Information Systems
BPA	business process automation
BPEL	Business Process Execution Language
BPM	business process management
BPMN	Business Process Modeling Notation
BPMS	business process management system
BPR	Business Process Reengineering
CCOR	Customer Chain Operations Reference Model
CEO	chief executive officer
CFO	chief financial officer
CIO	chief information officer
CKO	chief knowledge officer
CoE	Center of Excellence
COO	chief operating officer
COP	Community of Practice
CPO	chief process officer
CRM	customer relationship management
DCOR	Design Chain Operations Reference Model
DFSS	Design for Six Sigma
DMADV	Design, Measure, Analyze, Design Details, Verify
DMAIC	Design, Measure, Analyze, Improve, Control
DODAF	US Department of Defense Architecture Framework
EAI	enterprise application integration
EPC	event-driven process chain
ERP	enterprise resource planning
ETOM	Enhanced Telecom Operations Map
GRC	governance, risk, and compliance
HR	human resources
HSE	health, safety, and environmental
IT	information technology
ITIL	IT Infrastructure Library
KPI	key performance indicator
MRP	materials requirement planning
OEM	original equipment manufacturer
PAAS	platform as a service
PCF	process classification framework
PMBOK	Project Management Reference Model
PoPM	Process of Process Management
PPMS	process performance monitoring system
QA	quality assurance
QFD	quality function deployment
RACI	responsible, accountable, consulted, informed
RFID	radio frequency identification
RPH	Siemens Reference Process House
SAAS	software as a service
SCM	supply chain management
SCOR	Supply Chain Operations Reference Model
SOA	service-oriented architecture
TQM	Total Quality Management
VRM	Value Reference Model

Bibliography

American Productivity and Quality Center. "Using Process Frameworks and Reference Models to Get Real Work Done: Best Practices Report." APQC, 2011.

Bossidy, Larry, and Ram Charan. *Execution: The Discipline of Getting Things Done.* New York: Crown Business, 2002.

Brocke, Jan vom, and Michael Rosemann, eds. *Handbook on Business Process Management, Volumes 1 and 2.* Berlin: Springer-Verlag, 2010.

Carter, Sandy. *The New Language of Business: SOA & Web 2.0.* Upper Saddle River, NJ: IBM Press, 2007.

Champy, James. *X-Engineering the Corporation: Reinventing Your Business in the Digital Age.* New York: Warner Business Books, 2002.

Cheese, Peter, Robert J. Thomas, and Elizabeth Craig. *The Talent Powered Organization: Strategies for Globalization, Talent Management and High Performance.* London: Kogan Page, 2007.

Chowdhury, Subir. *Design for Six Sigma.* Chicago: Dearborn Trade, 2002.

Christensen, Clayton M., and Michael E. Raymour. *The Innovator's Solution: Creating and Sustaining Successful Growth.* Boston: Harvard Business School Press, 2003.

Collins, Jim. *Good to Great: Why Some Companies Make the Leap . . . and Others Don't.* New York: HarperCollins, 2001.

Cua, Kristy O., Kathleen E. McKone, and Roger G. Schroeder. "Relationships Between Implementation of TQM, JIT, and TPM and Manufacturing Performance." *Journal of Operations Management* 19 (2001): 675–94.

Davenport, Thomas H. *Mission Critical: Realizing the Promise of Enterprise Systems.* Boston: Harvard Business School Press, 2000.

Davila, Tony, Marc J. Epstein, and Robert Shelton. *Making Innovation Work: How to Manage It, Measure It, and Profit from It.* Upper Saddle River, NJ: Pearson, 2006.

De Feo, Joseph, and William Barnard. *Juran Institute's Six Sigma Breakthrough and Beyond: Quality Performance Breakthrough Methods.* New York: McGraw-Hill, 2004.

Deming, W. Edwards. "Out of the Crisis." MIT Center for Advanced Engineering Study, 1986.

Fettke, Peter, and Peter Loos. "Classification of Reference Models: A Methodology and Its Application." *Information Systems and E-Business Management* 1 (1): 35–53.

Fettke, Peter, and Peter Loos, eds. *Reference Modeling for Business Systems Analysis.* Hershey, PA: Idea Group, 2007.

Ficalora, Joseph P., and Lou Cohen. *Quality Function Deployment & Six Sigma.* 2nd ed. Upper Saddle River, NJ: Prentice Hall, 2009.

Fingar, Peter. *Extreme Competition: Innovation and the Great 21st Century Business Reformation.* Tampa, FL: Meghan-Kiffer, 2006.

Fleisch, Elgar, Oliver Christ, and Markus Dierkes. "Die betriebswirtschaftliche Vision des Internets der Dinge." In *Das Internet der Dinge: Ubiquitous Computing und RFID in der Praxis,* edited by Elgar Fleisch and Friedemann Mattern, 3–37. Berlin: Springer-Verlag, 2005.

Fleming, Maureen, Jeff Silverstein. "IDC MarketScape: Worldwide Business Process Platforms 2011 Vendor Analysis." Framingham, MA, 2011.

Franz, Peter. "Prioritizing Business Process Improvements to Maximize Agility." London: Accenture BPM Publication, 2011.

Franz, Peter, Mathias Kirchmer, and Michael Rosemann. "Value-Driven Business Process Management: Which Values Matter for BPM." Accenture and Queensland University of Technology, 2011.

Friedman, Thomas L. *The World Is Flat: A Brief History of the Twenty-First Century.* New York: Picador, 2005.

George, Mark O. *The Lean Six Sigma Guide to Doing More with Less: Cut Costs, Reduce Waste and Lower Your Overhead.* Hoboken, NJ: John Wiley & Sons, 2010.

George, Michael L., and Stephen A. Wilson. *Conquering Complexity in Your Business: How Wal-Mart, Toyota, and Other Top Companies Are Breaking Through the Ceiling on Profits and Growth.* New York: McGraw-Hill, 2004.

Hammer, Michael, and James Champy. *Reengineering the Corporation: A Manifesto for Business Revolution.* New York: HarperCollins, 1993.

Hammer, Michael, and Steven A. Stanton. *The Reengineering Revolution.* New York: HarperCollins, 1995.

Harmon, Paul. *Business Process Change: A Manager's Guide to Improving, Redesigning, and Automating Processes.* San Francisco: Morgan Kaufmann, 2003.

Harry, Mikel, and Richard Schroeder. *Six Sigma.* New York: Random House, 2000.

Imai, Masaaki. *Kaizen: Der Schluessel zum Erfolg der Japaner im Wettbewerb.* Munich: Langen/Müller, 1992.

Jost, Wolfram. *EDV-gestuetzte CIM Rahmenplanung.* Wiesbaden: Gabler, 1993.

Jost, Wolfram. "Vom CIO zum CPO." *Harvard Business Manager* (September 2004): 88–89.

Kirchmer, Mathias. *Business Process Oriented Implementation of Standard Software: How to Achieve Competitive Advantage Efficiently and Effectively,* 2nd ed. Berlin: Springer-Verlag, 1999.

Kirchmer, Mathias. "Competitive Advantage in an Era of Change: 11 Typical Business Situations Where Business Process Management Delivers Value." Philadelphia: Accenture BPM Publication, 2011.

Kirchmer, Mathias. *High Performance Through Process Excellence.* 2nd ed. Berlin: Springer-Verlag, 2011.

Kirchmer, Mathias. "The Process of Process Management: Delivering the Value of Business Process Management." Philadelphia: Accenture BPM Publication, 2011.

Kirchmer, Mathias, George Brown, and Herbert Heinzel. "Using SCOR and Other Reference Models for E-Business Process Networks." In *Business Process Excellence: ARIS in Practice,* edited by August-Wilhelm Scheer, Ferri Abolhassan, Wolfram Jost, and Mathias Kirchmer, 45–64. Berlin: Springer-Verlag, 2002.

Kirchmer, Mathias, Francisco Gutierrez, and Sigifredo Laengle. "Process Mining for Organizational Agility." *Industrial Management* (January/ February 2010): 19–24.

Kirchmer, Mathias, and August-Wilhelm Scheer. "Business Process Automation: Combining Best and Next Practices." In *Business Process Automation: ARIS in Practice,* edited by August-Wilhelm Scheer, Ferri Abolhassan, Wolfram Jost, and Mathias Kirchmer, 1–15. Berlin: Springer-Verlag, 2004.

Kirchmer, Mathias, and August-Wilhelm Scheer. "Change Management: Key for Business Process Excellence." In *Business Process Change Management: ARIS in Practice,* edited by August-Wilhelm Scheer, Ferri Abolhassan, Wolfram Jost, and Mathias Kirchmer, 1–14. Berlin: Springer-Verlag, 2003.

Krafcik, John F. "Triumph of the Lean Production System." *MIT Sloan Management Review* 30, no. 1 (Fall 1988): 41–52.

Lapkin, Anne. "The Seven Fatal Mistakes of Enterprise Architecture." Gartner Research publication, ID-Number: G00126144, February 22, 2005.

Majchrzak, Ann, Dave Logan, Ron McCurdy, and Mathias Kirchmer. "Four Keys to Managing Emergence." *MIT Sloan Management Review* 47, no. 2 (Winter 2006): 14–18.

McGovern, James, Scott W. Ambler, Michael E. Stevens, James Linn, Vikas Sharan, and Elias K. Jo. *A Practical Guide to Enterprise Architecture.* Upper Saddle River, NJ: Prentice-Hall, 2004.

Melenowsky, Michael J. "Business Process Management as a Discipline." Gartner Research, August 2006.

Morgan, Royston. "How to Do RACI Charting and Analysis: A Practical Guide." UK: Project Smart. Accessed September 26, 2011. http://www.projectsmart.co.uk.

O'Reilly, Tim. "What Is Web 2.0: Design Patterns and Business Models for the Next Generation of Software." September 30, 2005. http://oreilly.com/web2/archive/what-is-web-20.html.

O'Rourke, Carol, Neal Fishman, and Warren Selkow. *Enterprise Architecture Using the Zachman Framework.* Boston: Course Technology, 2003.

Porter, Michael E. *Competitive Strategy: Techniques for Analyzing Industries and Competitors.* New York: Free Press, 1998.

Pringle, Hamish, and William Gordon. *Brand Manners: How to Create the Self-Confident Organisation to Live the Brand.* Chichester, UK: John Wiley & Sons, 2001.

Rummler, Geary A., Alan J. Ramias, and Richard A. Rummler. *White Space Revisited: Creating Value Through Process.* San Francisco: Jossey-Bass, 2010.

Scheer, August-Wilhelm. *Business Process Engineering: Reference Models for Industrial Enterprises.* 2nd ed. Berlin: Springer-Verlag, 1994.

Scheer, August-Wilhelm. *ARIS: Business Process Frameworks.* 3rd ed. Berlin: Springer-Verlag, 2000.

Scheer, August-Wilhelm. *ARIS: Business Process Modeling.* 2nd ed. Berlin: Springer-Verlag, 1998.

Scheer, August-Wilhelm, Ferri Abolhassan, Wolfram Jost, and Mathias Kirchmer, eds. *Business Process Automation: ARIS in Practice.* Berlin: Springer-Verlag, 2004.

Scheer, August-Wilhelm, Ferri Abolhassan, Wolfram Jost, and Mathias Kirchmer, eds. *Business Process Change Management: ARIS in Practice.* Berlin: Springer-Verlag, 2003.

Scheer, August-Wilhelm, Ferri Abolhassan, Wolfram Jost, and Mathias Kirchmer, eds. *Business Process Excellence: ARIS in Practice.* Berlin: Springer-Verlag, 2002.

Sinur, Jim, and Janelle B. Hill. "Gartner Magic Quadrant for Business Process Management Suites." Gartner , Stamford, CT, 2010.

Snee, Ronald D., and Roger W. Hoerl. *Leading Six Sigma: A Step-by-Step Guide Based on Experience with GE and Other Six Sigma Companies.* Upper Saddle River, NJ: Pearson, 2003.

Spanyi, Andrew. *Business Process Management Is a Team Sport: Play It to Win!* Tampa, FL: Meghan-Kiffer, 2003.

Spanyi, Andrew. *More for Less: The Power of Process Management.* Tampa, FL: Meghan-Kiffer, 2006.

Supply Chain Council, ed. "Supply Chain Operations Reference Model: Plan, Source, Make, Deliver, Return." Version 8.0. Supply Chain Council, 2007.

Value Chain Group, ed. "Value Reference Model: VRM Methodology Coverage." Accessed July 31, 2011. http://www.value-chain.org/value-reference-model.

Vollner, Ken. "The EA View: BPM Has Become Mainstream." Forrester, October 2008.

Welch, Jack, and Suzy Welch. *Winning.* New York: HarperCollins, 2005.

White, Stephen A., and Derek Miers. *BPMN Modeling and Reference Guide.* Lighthouse Point, FL: Future Strategies, 2008.

Wilson, Chris, and Julie Short. "Magic Quadrant for Enterprise Architecture Tools." Gartner, Stamford, CT, October 28, 2010.

Woods, Dan. *Packaged Composite Applications.* Sebastopol, CA: O'Reilly Media, 2003.

Woods, Dan, and Thomas Mattern. *Enterprise SOA: Designing IT for Business Innovation.* Sebastopol, CA: O'Reilly Media, 2006.

Index

About the Authors

Peter Franz is the Managing Director for Business Process Management (BPM) at Accenture, responsible for the global team that helps clients translate strategy into execution using process as the critical link. Through Value-Driven BPM, Accenture helps organizations realize immediate value, deliver measureable results, and establish a lasting BPM capability. With more than 28 years experience in the areas of technology and the use of process to solve business problems—the two areas where BPM is converging today—he maintains a focus on balancing theory with realistic goals and concerns, and directs high-quality, pragmatic programs that drive real value for a roster of global clients. In leading Accenture's BPM practice, he champions thinking that achieves a customer-centered, cost-effective outcome in an increasingly information-intensive environment.

Mr. Franz has a Bachelor of Science degree in Computer Science and a Masters degree in Commerce from the University of the Witwatersrand in South Africa. He holds a Certificate of Production and Inventory Management from the American Production and Inventory Control Society (APICS). He is an active member of a number of professional organizations.

Dr. Mathias Kirchmer is Partner and Executive Director for Business Process Management (BPM) at Accenture. He leads the global BPM-Lifecycle Practice, as well as the program for the development of Accenture's BPM Reference Models. His special field of expertise is to establish BPM capabilities that deliver both immediate benefits as well as sustainable competitive advantages. Before joining Accenture, Dr. Kirchmer spent 18 years at IDS Scheer, a leading provider of business process excellence solutions, known for its BPM Software, the ARIS Platform.

Dr. Kirchmer is an affiliated faculty member of the Program for Organizational Dynamics of the University of Pennsylvania, a faculty member of the Business School of Widener University, Philadelphia, and a guest professor at the Universidad de Chile, Santiago. He is the author of numerous articles, whitepapers, and five books. The most recent book is *High Performance through Process Excellence* (Springer-Verlag, 2nd ed., 2011). Dr. Kirchmer holds a doctorate in Information Systems from Saarbrücken University (Germany), a Master in Business Administration and Computer Science from Karlsruhe Technical University (Germany), and a Master in Economics from Université Paris-Dauphine (France).

CPSIA information can be obtained
at www.ICGtesting.com
Printed in the USA
FFOW03n0741130416
23175FF